FOR THE LOVE OF
BENNY

FOR THE LOVE OF
BENNY

A Family Journey Wrapped Around the Delicate Fingers
of Their Special Needs Child

by
MARIETTA TROYER

Printed in the United States of America
Printed, bound and designed by The Herald Inc.

First Printing, 2017

ISBN: 978-0-692-96035-6

Published by:
Marietta Troyer

For information or comments, please contact:
Maynard & Marietta Troyer
15245 State Route 45
Lisbon, OH 44432
maynardtroyer@att.net

Blog: www.bennylovebennylife.com
Follow Benny on Instagram @throughbubbyseyes

DEDICATION

To Benny Boy.
The most beautiful soul of anyone I know.

TABLE OF CONTENTS

FOREWORD

This is a love story of a family's journey of being wrapped around the life of a special needs child. FOR THE LOVE OF BENNY embraces every fiber of life and leaves no emotions unturned. It deals with both the joys of triumph and the agonies of defeat. It deals with acceptance and rejection as well as the many whys and why nots. It is an inside look at a mother's tears, fears, and anguish that is openly exposed to the world so that we just might catch a glimpse and better understand. Written from the tender heart of a mother, it challenges the very core of our existence and makes us see a beauty and wisdom that can only be grasped by the heart.

We call them special needs children, but in reality they are God's special creation ordained to lead us into a fuller and richer understanding of genuine love with no conditions or demands. The daily journey of Benny will take you beyond the glorious heights of the highest mountains as you climb with him in his simple existence.

I have the privilege of knowing Benny personally and there is no greater joy than to be received by him with his hands clasped together as he lowers and tilts his head. He bows before all those he meets and makes you feel so royally special. Is this not how we should greet all that we meet?

THE LOVE OF BENNY will show you a deeper, richer and kinder love that only a special needs child can give. In a world filled with empty hearts craving love and acceptance, God created these special needs children as His special gift. God makes no mistakes but everything He creates has a special purpose. Our special needs children are a very special gift of love that is wrapped around the delicate fingers of a loving God and touches all mankind.

Sue Thomas
Inspiration of family award winning TV Series: SUE THOMAS: FBEye
and author of SILENT NIGHT and STAYING IN THE RACE
www.suethomasfbeye.com

ACKNOWLEDGMENTS

First of all, I acknowledge Jesus Christ, my Lord and Savior, who gave his life so that I may be free at last from bitterness. He holds and carries Maynard and me as we travel this mountain called Special Needs. Without the love of God, we would not be able to go on.

This book could not have been written without the cheer-leading of the closest individuals in my life. While I spent many hours, days and nights in my bedroom writing, those in my household stepped in and took over with Benny's care.

A very special and heartfelt thank you to my patient and kind husband, Maynard, and to three of my beautiful, giving daughters, Diana, Hannah and Samantha. You stuck with me through it all and graciously let me disappear into my writer's corner when I know you were weary and just wanted me to be there to help with Benny. God bless you!

Another thank you to my married daughter, Laurie, and her husband, Paul. Laurie, bless you for sending encouraging texts just as I was ready to give up. Thank you for listening to the voice of God when he prompted you to text Mom! To Paul, thank you for repeatedly asking about my book and reminding me to keep writing.

Thank you to my sisters, Ruby and Linda, for your honesty and advice. Your input and opinions are valuable to me.

Then there is Deborah. Whew! Where do I begin? Deborah not only edited my story, but she was also the midwife at Benny's birth. Her wisdom and love made the story of Benny priceless. I pray a blessing on your life, Deborah, for all your hard work. Although I feel Dutch is still the best, *ahem*, thank you for being honest with me and correcting all my too Dutchy phrases into proper English. I learned more about writing through your editing than I ever did in school. Your kindness and patience amaze me.

Sue Thomas, thank you for not only being a cheerleader but also for straightening me out when I needed it. I treasure the memories of sitting at your island over Chinese take-out and sparkling water, while you listened to my heart. You may be deaf but you don't miss a thing! You laughed and cried with me throughout the whole process, and even sent me home to rewrite a chapter, encouraging me to be more real and not to worry about sparing the dark details.

Benny, thank you for your life. It is your love and goodness that cheer me on every day. You are the total and complete inspiration of **For the Love of Benny.**

Hand drawn with love by Benny's sister, Samantha.

FOR THE LOVE OF
BENNY

ONE
Buggy Rides, Wedding Bells and Babies

THE FRISKY BROWN HORSE seemed to fly down the dusty gravel road as I gazed up at the starry night sky. With cap strings flapping in the breeze, my eight year old self was oblivious to the fact that we were sitting solidly behind one of the most down to earth, lowly, standard bred plugs in horse history. Star was a stubborn, but safe, horse. His mane seemed to flow in the breeze, as we slowly clopped across the rugged miles. We were on our way home from visiting Grandpas at their beautiful farm in the country.

"Dad!" I exclaimed, "Look at all those fire bugs! There must be a million, billion, trillion of them! Oh, I wish we could stop and catch some!"

The fields were literally alive and dancing with blinking fireflies as we made our trek home. Those bio-luminescent beauties were putting on a dazzling, summer night show fit for the queen of England. It was like hundreds of stars had fallen from the sky, twinkling magically to flit and hover over the freshly mowed alfalfa.

1

Although I wasn't raised on a farm, I did grow up Amish. I have many rich and rewarding experiences of tagging along in the horse drawn buggy every chance I got. Granted, some of those adventures were also wild and scary, such as when we had a horse with a will that rivaled a three year old spoiled child in a candy store in New York City.

One such horse, Perty, had the terrible ability to turn Sunday morning routines into ridiculous nightmares.

"Okay, kids, everybody get yourselves out onto the surrey. I'm bringing Perty out shortly," Dad would say. Tension was already crackling loud and clear and bouncing off the walls.

We all obediently grabbed our bonnets and shawls and scampered out to climb into the surrey. A buggy that had double seats was called a surrey, and once you had one, you were considered one of the larger families. Something like when a young couple goes from a Camaro to a minivan. It takes the ego down about two or three notches, but the blessing of children far outweighs the gigantic means of transportation you now need.

By now, my whole body was bristling with anxiety. I saw Dad coming with Perty and I quickly put my head down on my lap and covered my ears so I wouldn't know or see anything that would befall us until it was over. It was the best way to deal with the awful fear that clutched my tummy.

We all sat there on pins and needles. It was a marathon sprint each time. Would Dad make it onto the surrey or would he be left behind as his mortified troops sailed down the road without him? The minute Perty realized she was hitched, she took off, and poor Dad had to kind of aim and shoot into the surrey like his life depended on it. If Perty had tires, they would have squealed and left a trail of thick black smoke. We lived right beside a busy highway, but it didn't matter to her whether there might be a car coming or not. She was hitched and it was time to run flat out immediately. And so we did. Until Dad had enough of this monkey business and we acquired Star. It was the best thing ever to be able to get ready for church without the anxious scurrying just to get rolling down State Route 62.

But even more terrifying was when I met and married Maynard, and he not only drove insane horses, he delighted in it! The wilder the horse, the happier the man.

How did I land such an amazing husband that danced to the tune of a lunatic horse? Let me tell you the story...

One cold winter evening, when I was 17 years old, my brother and I made our way to a tiny neighboring village with a large ice skating pond where all the young people came together to glide across the ice and make eyes at each other. I looked across the sheet of frozen water and there he was in all his glory. My knight in shining armor was making eyes and smiling at me!

We started dating, and got married three years later. In our dreams we would be perfect and live happily ever after, never falling out of love, and we were going to have a few really cute, awesome, funny, blond haired, blue eyed little human beings coming along behind us, in our very own make and model.

We planned that our fortune would be made from raising the most astounding Percheron horses that humankind ever did see. We did have the most precious, amazing children, but never did make that fortune breeding Percheron horses. Sorry to burst your bubble, newly married, energetic couple embarking on the ride of your life!

Three months after we were married I became very ill. I puked at every smell invented by life. Fall leaves? Gag. Coffee? Gag. Melting butter? Gag. Hamburger frying in a pan?

3

Scream and gag both. Oh, I was running around in search of toilets all across the earth, emptying my stomach completely at every turn, because of a world suddenly encased with horrific scents. You guessed it. That first awesome little heartbeat was growing inside of me, and we had our first beautiful baby exactly ten days after our first anniversary. Diana was perfect in every way, and we enjoyed her so much.

Our happy little family settled down to life on the farm. Making hay in the warm July months, and hunkering down during the long, cold winters, drinking hot chocolate made from scratch, and devouring gallons of rich, homemade ice cream, made from the abundant proceeds of our Jersey cow named Daisy.

As I was cheerfully doing laundry one day, the smell of the fabric softener suddenly turned my stomach inside out, and thirteen months after Diana was born, another little girl was added to our family. She really did have blond hair, blue eyes, and even curls! Laurie was flawless, the same as Diana, and wow, were we ever proud of our adorable little clan! They were the cutest, rosy-cheeked girlies I have ever seen.

"I am going out to hitch the horse for your doctor appointment. I will take Diana with me while you get Laurie ready," stated Maynard as he held Diana's hand and went out the door.

He was a great daddy, this knight of mine.

I watched as they paused together and looked up into the blue sky, intently observing something.

"What is it, Diana?" I heard him say as they regarded the effortless glide of a black helicopter until it was out of sight.

"It's a choo-choo train!" exclaimed Diana in wonder and delight.

Maynard erupted into laughter as they made their way out to the barn to harness the horse.

I stepped out with Laurie a few minutes later, but halted in great fear and trembling when I saw the very feisty, unpredictable Morgan riding horse hitched to the buggy instead of our usual faithful, albeit, highly energetic, standard bred gelding. Tanya had her head held high, allowing her the ability to peer at the looming black buggy that followed her every move. The whites of her eyes were visible as she rolled them back in panic stricken terror, in order to keep the terrifying new object in view. Maynard hung on to the bridle as Tanya made a valiant effort to prance and dance away to escape her dilemma. I could imagine her thinking, *These humans are crazy. What bewildering task are they asking me to do now? I just want to go back to my stall and munch on some fresh oats. No, wait; let me instead give them the ride of their life. Yes, that's what I'll do!*

"No, I am not doing this. I am not getting in that buggy. Forget it." I was petrified and pretty upset.

"You have to. Buddy threw his shoe, and we can't take him."

"What about one of your dad's horses? Let's take one of his! Please?" We lived at home on Maynard's parents' farm. Their fuddy-duddy, extremely docile mare was looking most desirable compared to the reckless ride I was sure we were about to experience. I could hear my voice coming out in short breathless bursts.

"No, we are taking Tanya," insisted Maynard. "I've wanted to see how she will handle a buggy for a long time anyway. Come on, it will be fun."

Upon seeing my terrified expression, he rolled his eyes. "Okay, I will take a spin around the drive before you get on. Stay right there."

A spin he said. It was more like a rodeo show. They lurched and jerked around and around in circles. Suddenly, Tanya realized that the black thing behind her was not going to kill her, and she calmed down enough to take us to town, head held high, parading down the country roads like a boss. Away we went, steady by jerks. The sound of my strangled yells could be heard throughout the fields of busy farmers as we went careening by. But we made it to town and even back home, all living and breathing to tell the story.

Our lives settled down to some semblance of normality, where I didn't get sick, or have any more babies for four years. Then one day another delightful little girl was brought into our world. By this time we had made the decision to purchase our own car, and we made a flying trip to the hospital. The insane speeds at which we traveled will not be mentioned here for the entire world to see. The violent shaking of the vehicle did not help my awkward position of sitting, laying, standing in the back seat. Between overwhelming contractions I breathlessly yelled,

"Slow down! I'm fine! We'll make it, I promise!"

Maynard kept the pedal to the medal, if you know what I mean, and upon arrival at the hospital, the energetic nurses made mad dashes everywhere to get me into a bed quickly.

"Where are you going, Mr. Troyer?" shouted the frantic nurse, when she spied Maynard leaving the room.

"I'm headed out to park the car. It's still under the entrance roof, running and with the doors open." said Maynard.

"You ain't going anywhere," she smiled firmly. "We are having ourselves a baby right now!"

And just like that, we had ourselves another baby. There she was in all her newborn infant glory, wailing in protest at the rude, harsh awakening into this bright, cold world. Hannah was beautiful with a head of dark hair, and a hefty set of lungs. There was only one glitch. As I looked down at my precious baby, I noticed a mass of something on her stomach. Oh, no, what in all the earth?

"What is that?" I asked, panic and dread all crowding into my voice which was still exhausted from my last intense hour of life. "What is that on her stomach?"

I can still so clearly see the doctor's calm assuring face and tone of voice as he stated, "She will be just fine. It's only her intestines. We will make sure it will all be taken care of. See? I can push them all back inside, and when she cries they all come wiggling back out! Don't you worry one bit."

She was born with her intestines on the outside! She was transferred to Akron Children's Hospital immediately, and scheduled for surgery.

Prior to surgery, the surgeon asked us, "Would you like for me to make her a designer belly button? It's my favorite thing to do! If I don't make her one, she will always be without a belly button!"

"I'm trying to picture a person without one and it's not coming together for me," I replied with a hint of laughter.

Maynard chuckled and agreed.

The doctor then proceeded to show us with a napkin just how he would design this very special part of Hannah. The seamstress inside of me understood the technique right away. It was quite an amazing work of talented art, and we quickly agreed that a belly button would be a great idea.

Hannah was in surgery at a mere ten hours old. The surgeon repaired everything. He stuffed all her intestines inside where they belonged, and made her a man-made belly button.

Everything went well and we were home in our cozy abode in four days, loving our little family of girls.

"Look, girls! That baby on the screen is your sister or brother." we were eager for the girls to meet our fourth baby as we all gathered around the ultra sound in the dimly lit room.

"He/she is tiny," observed the nurse, "Maybe he/she is due later than you thought. Oh my, look! The baby is waving at you. I can't believe it; it appears exactly like she is saying, *hello there, nice to meet you all!* That is very special."

We left the doctor's office, excited and chattering about our new baby coming in February, and how cute it was that she waved her tiny hand at us.

The winter months that year were unusually cold. Ice storms blew in constantly, making Maynard's milk route with his big truck very difficult and treacherous. No matter the weather, cows will still produce milk and that milk needs hauled whether it is sunny and warm or cold and bleak. He maneuvered icy lanes and un-plowed snow covered country roads daily to reach the Amish farmers in New Wilmington and did his best to deliver it to the cheese house, ensuring their income.

Then one especially brisk day, fifteen months after Hannah was born, we found ourselves racing towards a birthing center. Upon arrival we settled in and the plump midwife, Lucille, examined me. She glanced over at Deborah, her apprentice, before quietly delivered heart shattering news in a calm and loving voice,

"Something is wrong. I'm so sorry, but I can't find a heartbeat."

"No heartbeat?" I faltered. Feeling faint, I collapsed back on the pillow. Despair and hopelessness washed over me like never before.

"You mean I will give birth to a dead baby?" I queried incredulously.

My befuddled brain tried to communicate to my heart the event unfolding right before my eyes.

I looked over at Maynard, still in his denim overalls from being on his milk truck, and saw sadness and grief wash over his whole being as it began to sink in.

A contraction hit me full force and left me no room to think for a minute. I came back to reality as it subsided.

"There is no way I am going through this whole ordeal and then delivering a dead baby, Maynard! I can't do it, and I won't do it." I said emphatically, as if that was all there was to it.

Stillborn. How I hated that choice of words. It sounded so...well...final, so still. I lay there in agony for a few hours. My contractions slowed to a stop as my body refused to give birth.

I was dimly aware that Maynard, my pillar of strength, had crawled right up onto the bed behind me, wrapped his arms around me and prayed out loud along with Deborah and Lucille, asking God to release the grip of fear that was binding me.

I don't remember exactly how it left. I didn't see any great white flashes of lightening, or divine powers from above zipping their way through the room. All I know is a great, warm peace enfolded me like a blanket and my will was in the Father's hands.

"Okay, I'm ready. But please will you take my baby right away and look at it before you give her to me? If the baby is deformed or already decayed I want to be warned first," I whispered into the hushed atmosphere.

My very still Sara Emmilene was born moments later. Lucille gently wrapped her in a blanket and whisked her off to the nursery to examine her.

"It's a girl. She's not deformed or decayed. She's beautiful and she has black hair," Lucille spoke kindly.

"Isn't she sweet?" asked Lucille as she placed her in my arms. "I put her in this soft little basket for you. She will be easier to hold this way."

I was awestruck. It seemed so surreal. Although it was grievously sad, it was also beautiful at the same time.

Sara was full term but she only weighed in at 2 pounds. So precious! As I held her in my trembling arms and stroked her very cool cheek with the back of my fingers, I marveled that God should have chosen us to receive this tiny gift, only to give her back to glory right away. Our sweet Sara Emmilene, gone so quickly, into the arms of Jesus!

It was a tragically heartbreaking time of our life. To bury a tiny baby is almost unbearable. A wise person shared with us that we could choose to let this experience make us bitter or better. With many tears and soul searching, we chose the latter. We can look back now and thank God for this soul-crushing experience.

We know we will meet our Sara Emmilene again beyond heavens gates, when she comes running and skipping, with black curls flowing in the heavenly breeze, to welcome us home. Until then we will treasure in our hearts the memory of her waving at us from the womb.

Prayers were sent heavenward fifteen months later as with great trepidation we brought our rainbow baby into the world. Babies born shortly after the loss of a previous baby, due to miscarriage, stillbirth, or death in infancy, are called rainbow babies. This is because a rainbow follows a storm and signifies hope of the blessing to come.

Becoming pregnant soon after losing Sara brought an onslaught of emotions, and I can tell you they were not all positive. I felt a tremendous sense of self-doubt and guilt at times. I was afraid that others would think that I was over Sara, or that I was trying to replace her. I was afraid that in some way I was dishonoring Sara's memory.

But Samantha Faith arrived kicking and screaming, as if to announce, *"Hello, Mom! Hi, Dad! I am here. I am safe. Do not worry or cry anymore, Mommy. Your prayers were heard. I am vibrant and healthy! I am as cute as a button and I even have a head of hair that will soon need braids, just like you asked!"*

With that, all the misgivings, anxiety, and fears completely dissipated and our hearts were triumphantly renewed and healed.

I realized that feeling pure joy at the birth of Samantha did not mean that Sara would be forgotten. Such a devastating loss could never be erased from my heart. Rather, Samantha carried the torch of the love I will always have for Sara. Only when I held my precious, thriving, newborn baby in my arms, could I fully understand the term rainbow baby. Samantha was my rainbow after a devastating storm.

People remarked on what an extra beautiful baby she was. I smiled and thought; *Mary kept all these things and pondered them in her heart.* I had begged and cried all throughout my pregnancy for a healthy baby...and a really cute one. After every prayer I said something like this,

And please make my baby the cutest baby anyone has ever seen. You took Sara away, it's the least you could do, God.

Do people even talk to God like that? Should we even speak that way to God? I don't know for sure, but I did, and he answered my prayer pretty directly. Even I was shocked, but my faith was strengthened. Did God know we would need a faith boost once we had Benny, and chose to give us what we asked, so we could look back and know he answers prayers? I believe so! I believe God knew our faith would be severely tested and that he would seem far away. Very soon in the future there would be days when no words would come forth and all we could was groan.

Be encouraged, though, if you are reading this, and indeed,

God feels far away at the moment. He is actually right there. You may be hurting too much to even comprehend how he is carrying you and giving you the grace to go on. The best part about it is that he was like as we are, and he understands! He gets it that he seems far away, but he will not hit you over the head with a hammer for your lack of trust. He is a great God, and desires us to call on him in the day of trouble. If you are too troubled to call, just send the message in your heart. He hears. He knows. He understands.

TWO
Life Before Benny

HOMESCHOOLING WAS IN FULL SWING. For a mother, it was like having two full time jobs. I will not even try to sugar coat it. It was hard work, but immensely satisfying. First, the girls learned their ABC's; then these letters would start to form words; the words became sentences; and then, of all things, the sentences turned into stories. To see the light bulbs go on in the girls' minds was rewarding to witness. Hence, I produced four little bookworms.

The older girls were always teaching the younger ones new lessons from school. One day Laurie took it upon herself to teach Hannah about capital punishment. How she settled on this subject was a mysterious wonder.

"Mom, I can't believe it! Laurie said if someone murders a person, the police hang them on a telephone wire and shoot them! Is that true, Mom?"

Even the flapping laundry I was taking off the line seemed to freeze mid air in horrified shock as I whirled around to face Hannah's bulging eyes.

"No, no, Hannah," I burst out laughing. "But they use capital punishment in the United States."

I could barely contain the giggles that wanted to erupt from deep within. Hang them on a telephone wire, indeed. Someone had their "wires" crossed. *Now where is Laurie hiding?*

"What's capital punishment, Mom?" asked Hannah.

So I explained it the best I could. What a terrible and controversial thing. But it is a government sanctioned practice in the country we live in, and my students will hear about it sometime so it may as well come from me.

"Oh, Mom, that is just awful. I can't believe those people could be so mean!"

I agreed it was a very unpleasant thing, and very sad that people murder to begin with.

"I sure am glad I don't live in that country," Hannah breathed a big sigh of relief.

Who is her teacher? Oh yes, it's me! But she just said...

"Hannah, dear, come here! You do live in the United States of America."

"But I thought we live in Ohio?"

"Yes, in Columbiana, in Ohio, inside the United States!"

"Oh." She mulled on that for awhile then stated, "Well, Mom, I am going to make sure I never murder anyone."

I assured her this was the best idea ever as she happily skipped away to feed her pet goat, Mocha, the biting dog, Rufus, her cat, Charlie, our two horses, Ginny and Dixie, and none other than an adored chicken named Goldilocks.

Although the classroom may be dismissed, a home school mom is never done teaching. Especially when her own students don't realize they live in the USA!

We fell into a good routine and around noon, our ears would perk to the sound of Maynard's big truck Jake-braking up to our driveway. It was music to all the females, both large and small, inside our household. Every single day, he came rolling down the blacktop highway exactly the same way. I could hear his growling diesel engine about a quarter mile away as he started down shifting with absolutely perfect timing. Each gear had a melodious note of its own. He would come gliding gracefully and precisely up to our lane, then slowly and carefully steer that Freight-liner onto our long gravel driveway. My master truck driving man then gently purred his way in, put that big, box truck in reverse, and maneuvered competently into his faithful parking spot. *He is my man; the milk man. No one could ever drive that truck like he does. I am so proud of him.*

Along with all these lovely sounds, there was also the sound of four wildly cheering little girls running carefree out the long narrow sidewalk towards the old red barn where the truck would finally roll to a stop. They were delighted to have their beloved daddy home, and did he bring a sweet treat from the cheese house?

Maynard hauled can milk for the Amish in New Wilmington, and then delivered it to the Middlefield Cheese House. His route consisted of 32 small family farms and he would stop and load their warm milk cans in order to get them to the cheese factory as quickly as possible.

These Amish still use the stainless steel milk cans. Each can held ten gallons of frothy white milk, and weighed 100 pounds when full.

My man, the milk man, really got into the swing of things and was able to stack those heavyweights three high.

The industrious farmers and their hard working families had milked the cows by hand in the wee hours of the morning, ensuring that it was ready to go when my man, the milk man, pulled up to the first farm at 5:00 a.m.

At one point, Maynard hired one of the young Amish boys to help load the milk on his route. He bought Amos breakfast at McDonalds every morning. Amos always got the exact same thing. Two super sized value meals gave him two sausage sandwiches, two enormous root beers and two hash brown patties. Upon each sandwich he applied two whole salt packets. The hash browns received the same treatment as the sandwiches; two whole packets of salt each.

"These fish are so good," Amos would say, as he vigorously bit into the salt encrusted hash brown. His insides must be as sturdy as the Dead Sea where it is so salty that all objects float and nothing ever sinks.

Playing along, Maynard always replied, "Yep, these fish are good. Hey, Amos, wanna wear my hat today?"

"Ya, sure," cackled Amos in delightful anticipation.

As they rolled away from McDonalds, they switched hats on many occasions. Maynard wore the Amish, black, broad rimmed, felt hat, and drove that milk truck like he owned the highway, while Amos wore Maynard's bill cap, and devoured *"fish"* like nobody's business. I'm sure it was quite a comical spectacle!

To this day, when we bite into a McDonalds hash brown patty, we say, "Mmm, these fish are good!" In Amos' defense, with a little imagination, they do taste like fish. There. Feel free to laugh at me!

The girls often took turns to get up insanely early and ride along on the route. I'm talking the 3:00 a.m. unearthly hour in the morning kind of early. They enjoyed being out on the country farms.

"Laurie, wake up, we are at Rover's farm. See if he will smile today!" Maynard grinned, as he gently roused her from her slumber.

"What? Oh!" Laurie pounced up out of the ball she was curled up in and rolled down her window to peer down at the friendly dog. "Good morning, Rover, you got a smile for me today?"

Rover didn't disappoint. He showed all his teeth and grinned like a cat with a mouse. His whole body waved back and forth as he wagged his tail like a dolphin at sea.

The best part, though, was to end up at the awesome Middlefield Cheese House where there were shelves laden with all manner of delicious candy. Wide-eyed, the girls would carefully choose from the variety of fudgy chocolate, peppermint, lollipops, licorice or caramel to bring home and share with their sisters.

One warm day in June, when we were out picking the first fresh strawberries from our large garden, a young man puttered into the lane in his green pickup truck.

After introductions were made, the young man announced, "I am here to buy your milk route. Is it for sale?"

Maynard looked up in surprise, "I guess it can be, if the price is right."

And just like that, after a few more conversations and meetings, the big milk truck purred quietly out our gravel driveway for the last time. We all stood on the porch, wincing just a little bit as the diesel engine revved up, followed by the hesitant, grinding sound of each gear.

"He needs lots of practice with those gears," commented Maynard. "But I bet he'll have it mastered within a few days."

"No one will ever drive that truck like you did, Maynard," I mused, looping my arm through his.

We enjoyed gardening, canning, cooking and baking. When we weren't doing school, we spent much of our time in the kitchen, putting to practice our rich, Amish heritage.

It was my joy to see the delight on Maynard's face when he would walk into the kitchen and there would be hot cinnamon rolls cooling on the table. Another favorite was homemade bread fresh out of the oven with Amish peanut butter slathered most generously to cover every square inch of the piece of bread. One must never leave even one spec uncovered.

How can peanut butter be Amish? I don't know how, except that it must have been created by the Amish! It is a mixture of peanut butter, light corn syrup, and marshmallow creme. That's all. It is non-Amish products all mixed together into a gooey mess creating a delicacy to spread on your slice of bread. It is so unbelievably scrumptious that you should be sure to be in a seated position when take your first bite, or you might fall and do yourself harm.

One day after we had sold the milk route, and Maynard had just come home from his new construction job, we sat down to fresh coffee and hot cinnamon rolls just out of the oven.

"Why is that coffee so horrible? That is the worst brew I've ever tasted. Eww! It stinks, too! Don't these cinnamon rolls taste funny, as well?" I ran to the bathroom and emptied my stomach.

"Honey, two plus two equals four. Perfectly wonderful coffee stinks. Melt in your mouth cinnamon rolls have a weird taste. You just threw up...get it?" He burst out laughing.

"That's not even funny," I glared at him with mock disgust. Could it be? The realization hit me that, yes, it could very well be. How exciting! Would we have a boy this time?

"When are you ever going to have a boy child, Maynard? You need a boy," well meaning friends would say.

"A boy would be great," Maynard would reply, shrugging nonchalantly. "We love our girls, though, so I don't see how it could be much different."

It was slightly annoying for us to have it constantly thrown into our face. It did not matter to us if we had another pink blanket. We wouldn't change a single one of our precious girls

18

into boys had we the power to do so.

As it turns out, one humid July day, in two thousand and three, as the tornado sirens were going off in town, that little blue blanket announced his presence into our lives. A miracle boy child was born to the Troyer family.

What we didn't know at the time is that in a sense, we were 'born' as well. We were born into a brand new world where a tiny little baby named Benny would become our master teacher.

THREE

A Boy Child is Born

"MY BABY, MY BABY," I breathed into the dimly lit room of our home. Delivery was over, joy of all joys, and I heard my baby's first cry. It was not a loud boisterous cry, but it didn't worry me.

"Yes, your baby," Deborah, my midwife, jubilantly stated as she nimbly cleared his mouth and nostrils of any mucus obstruction, "It's a boy!"

"It's a boy? Praise the Lord!" Maynard was ecstatic and could hardly contain the excitement wanting to explode from his heart. "I can't believe it's a boy!"

"Oh, my goodness!" I laughed, not only in relief from the trauma of birth, but also from the absolute shock of learning we had a baby boy. "I don't even know how to raise a boy but I will learn! Wait till we tell the girls!"

I watched as Deborah ran her fingers up and down my baby's chest, and listened intently with her stethoscope.

"Is he okay? Why are you doing that? Is he breathing right? Can I hold him? Hey, look at his ears! Are they deformed?" I was starting to feel uneasy.

Deborah kept listening and checking his heartbeat and air flow through his lungs. She seemed a bit puzzled.

"I think he will be fine. He's acting a bit like a preemie, though. Are you sure you had your dates right?" she asked.

"Yes, I'm positive we had the correct dates." I answered confidently.

"Okay, well he seems a little lethargic and his muscle tone is poor. He doesn't have any eyebrows. Just like a preemie. See how his ears were folded straight forward flat on the side of his face? I can flip them back where they belong and they stay right there. Like there is no muscle tone; similar to how a preemie would be. Notice how his hands and feet are floppy too?"

Maynard leaned in closer and added, "Yeah his feet lay straight up on his legs, and his hands lay straight down against his arms. Honey, look at this. How strange that he can do that. Is he severely double jointed?"

Deborah shook her head, "No, he is not double jointed. It's poor muscle tone. He needs some good nutrition in his stomach and he will gain strength and his muscle tone will develop."

She wrapped him up and placed him in my arms.

"There's your baby, mama."

I held this dear sweet new baby of mine and inhaled his baby scent. The smell of a newborn baby is intoxicating to a new mom. A new car smell is nice. A new baby smell is out-of-this-world-awesome. It all needs to be captured while it's there, because it lasts only a few days, and I can never get enough of it.

His face was perfectly round and surrounded by mounds of black shiny hair.

"You are so cute, little baby boy. We are naming you Benjamin Eric. We love you so much. You have really long skinny fingers, son. We will get you fed, and gaining weight and growing in no time." I crooned into his soft black hair and inhaled his scent again.

"Okay, little sweet man, it's time to see how much you weigh," murmured Deborah against his sweet baby cheeks as she carefully placed him inside her bag that hung off a scale. We all laughed as one skinny foot busted out of the bag as if to say, *Catch me if you can, I'm the Ginger Bread Man!*

"How much did your other babies weigh?" Deborah queried. "Because he is only a mere 5 pounds and 12 ounces and he is three days overdue. I wonder why his weight is so low? Well, no matter, you are not getting out of your bath, Benjamin Eric. Let's get you all spiffed up for the ladies that will be coming shortly to spoil you to pieces. Did you know that you have four sisters, Benny? Yes, you do. And you will have them all wrapped around your fingers in about two seconds, I promise."

I loved how Deborah spoke to Benjamin. *She is the best of the best*, I thought as I watched her carefully gather him up and whisk him away for a bath. The electricity was still off, so Maynard heated some water and they proceeded to bathe Benny, beneath the flickering candles and the flashlights gleaming to shed any light we had. Oh, I hoped the electricity would soon come back.

"Here's your chlorophyll, Marietta. Drink it for strength and sustenance," announced Deborah as she walked back into the room, carrying both a sparkling clean Benjamin and a glass of green chlorophyll. It was a drink she gave to all her new moms.

"Hey, where are you? What are you doing up? Get back to bed or at least sit down!"

We laughed as she guided me back to the couch.

"I feel so good! I always get a new wind after giving birth. That is, when I'm not passed out on the floor." I declared, provoking a horrified expression out of Deborah.

"What are you talking about? You have a history of passing out after giving birth and I didn't know about it?" retorted Deborah apprehensively.

"Only for my first two births. This is my sixth baby, so I think it's safe to say that is a thing of the past," I replied mischievously.

I noticed Deborah speaking quietly to Heather, her birth assistant, a few minutes later as she was handing Benjamin over to her. I couldn't hear what she said, but I noticed that Heather had the stethoscope ready and kept listening and stimulating his chest every so often. A shadow of disquiet went over my heart, but I shrugged it off.

Heather was invaluable. Throughout my entire labor, I had walked back and forth from the kitchen to the schoolroom right up until the dreaded pushing started while Heather had sat graciously on the living room floor, quietly strumming her guitar through it all. It had set the tone for a calm birth. When I finally landed in bed, just minutes before birth, she rubbed my back just right as I hummed some kind of melody in my last "out of mind state" minutes before birth.

In those last moments I kept chanting over and over to myself, "Jesus on the Cross. Jesus on the Cross."

When Maynard's Dad fought a heroic battle with cancer, he had told us that the only way to bear the pain was to think about the even greater torment Jesus suffered.

This spoke so directly to my heart that I decided to try it at childbirth. It actually made the pain less to repeat this phrase over and over. By the time I was done, there was no doubt in anyone's mind that a man called Jesus had died on a cross somewhere. Or maybe only the pillow heard it, since I was face planted squarely into it. Don't ask me how it worked, but I would do it that way all over again. In the past, sometimes, in those last minutes, other things had come forth out of my mouth that I was dreadfully ashamed of later. In order to preserve my dignity and reputation, there will be no need to elaborate or give more information at this time.

Although Maynard does get a good laugh when he starts in, "Remember when Diana was born and you told the nurse..."

Shush! Not going there on paper!

"I'm going to call my co-pastor and tell him the good news!" exclaimed Maynard as he reached for the phone. "He can start a hotline to let the church know there's a brand new brother in the fellowship, born during a severe thunderstorm with no electricity but only flashlights and candles! Then I will go pick up the girls from Jon and Ellie's house."

I overheard Maynard on the phone, giving the details about our newborn son and how the electricity was still off. Our co-pastor spoke loudly enough that I could hear from my position on the couch on the other side of the room.

"Congratulations on the miracle of your first son! But I hear the electricity could be off for a whole day yet. Let me see what I can do to help," offered Eldon kindly.

"Oh, no! Really? Okay, see what you come up with while I go get the girls," replied Maynard as he headed out the door with a spring to his step to fetch his princesses. Jon and Ellie were some of our best friends who lived only a few miles down the road, so I knew he and the girls would be back soon.

Moments later the van pulled in and four girls bounded gleefully out of the vehicle and came dashing into the house with smiles as wide as the Ohio River.

"Mom, I can't believe I have a brother!" exclaimed Laurie as she descended on Benjamin, beaming with pride and delight.

"Can I hold him first? I'm the oldest," Diana reminded us with a twinkle in her eye.

"You sure may," I answered tearfully. "You go ahead and love him to pieces and take turns holding him."

And so they did. I watched with a fulfilled heart as they lavished love and adoration on the newest member of the family. They all took turns brushing his hair to a shiny sheen and kissing his cheeks over and over.

"Hey! Now we aren't an all-girl family anymore," stated Diana.

"I think we should sing his song now that we are all here. We sang it to him all the time before birth. Now that he's arrived, let's sing it again." announced Maynard as he gathered his lady-troops.

We all sat on the bed surrounding Benjamin and sang him "his" song.

"Little Miracle" by Mary Rice Hopkins

"I'm a little miracle all put together well
Designed by my Father with a price too high to sell
I'm different from my brothers, (sisters) yet unique as I can be
You know that I am special 'cause there's only one of me."

Chorus:
"Miracle! I'm a miracle
I think that you'll agree, I'm unique as I can be
Miracle! I'm a miracle
You know that I am special 'cause there's only one of me."

"You know that I was thought about before the world began
God the Father made me with his own two loving hands
From the top of my head to the bottom of my feet
He gave me ten fingers and he even made my seat"...Chorus

God works in mysterious ways. How could we have possibly known that the words of this song would so accurately describe our Benny? We had sung it to him that very first time Deborah had applied the Doppler and we heard his tiny heart beating. We sang it to him almost every day of my pregnancy after that, and whenever we prayed for him during family devotions.

And now we were holding him in our arms and singing it again. Our family was perfect. We couldn't have been happier.

We all looked up as we heard the distinct sound of a diesel truck with the logo, *Goods Electric*, pulling into the yard. Our co-pastor was right behind in his trusty farm truck. As Maynard stepped outside into the soggy aftermath of the storm, a kind looking man came strolling up to the front door with Eldon.

"Hello! My name is Daniel Good. I hear congratulations are in order, and that you don't have electricity? I have come with a generator big enough to power your whole house, and we will be happy to set it up for you."

"Oh, wow, how kind! Sure! That would be awesome," replied Maynard happily.

Wonder of wonders, moments later the whole house purred to life as all electronics fired up their engines again and we had ourselves some electricity.

A brisk knock on the door brought Ellie and her children. She also brought some of the most amazing food on earth. The meal was complete with homemade bread, fried chicken, mashed potatoes and gravy, corn and peanut butter pie.

The food was oh, so delicious, and it felt so good to be spoiled and I was ravenous. After all, I had worked pretty hard all day.

"I just had to bring a gift for your first boy," she stated excitedly as she held up a tiny pair of bright red rain galoshes that were too adorable for words.

His first little pair of boots. In my mind I pictured him stomping muddy tracks across my newly washed kitchen floor. Little did I know his tiny feet would never stomp through mud to make dreadful tracks across my floors.

We all went to bed that night with thankful happy hearts.

Deborah and Heather had gone home with promises to return in 24 hours to make sure all was well.

When they came back the next evening I was very troubled.

"Benjamin has not eaten even one drop," I announced worriedly. "He won't latch on and feed for me."

Deborah was alarmed and went to work immediately, securing a bottle to see what we could do.

"Did you do any pumping so I can have breast milk?" she asked, concern crowding into her voice.

"Yes, I do have a little bit," I answered. "Maybe an ounce?"

"Okay, let's see what he does with that. And I suggest seeing a lactose consultant for help in getting him started. I am leaving for North Carolina tomorrow, so I won't be available to keep checking up on him," informed Deborah. I felt a little twinge of fear attach itself to my ankle and start gnawing away.

It was no small feat, but we got him to take that one ounce. I felt much better after that.

"If he won't latch on, you need to be pumping and giving it to him with a bottle. He must get some fluids in him or he will dehydrate," Deborah instructed before she went out the door.

I went to the hospital the very next day to get help from the lactation consultant. And this is how we rolled. Every day I tried to get him to latch on. Every day he would not latch on. Every day I faithfully pumped my breast milk like a fat Jersey cow. It was insanely frustrating and difficult and I became very disheartened about it. Nothing seemed to help.

He didn't seem to have much interest in eating, even with

a bottle. It took so long for him to drink two ounces of milk, that by the time he was done it was almost time to start another feeding. During the day this wasn't so bad, but during the night it was unbearably exhausting. I noticed that a lot of his milk ran out the sides of his mouth, and also that there were always droplets of sweat on his brow when he drank a bottle. I passed it off as hot summer days and that I was probably overdressing him.

"Maynard, what do you think about taking Benjamin in for a well baby check?" I tentatively questioned, after another despairing day of barely getting Benjamin to eat. It was consuming me. "I just have this little feeling of trouble looking over my shoulder all the time. He won't latch on and nurse, he doesn't take the bottle willingly, and he never bobs his head to look around like my other babies did. I would feel better to take him and make sure everything is okay. Maybe the doctor can help."

"Yes, I think that would be okay. Just be prepared for stinky home birth questions." he warned.

"I know. I will be very respectful. Don't worry," I replied, relieved that he had so readily agreed with me. I made an appointment immediately for the next day.

Benjamin had turned the two week old mark and his feeding issues had not improved. I felt such a great weight that had a giant dinosaur settled down on my chest, the burden would not have been any less. I lived and breathed this unsettling dilemma and claimed it as my own, walking each day in worry and dread. I knew that a vibrant healthy baby would eat. I knew that you almost can't keep enough food in most babies, and that they scream when they're not fed. Benjamin did none of this.

The jingling of the phone roused me from my troubled thoughts. It was my family asking if it was okay if they came to meet Benjamin that evening. I was overjoyed! They lived almost two hours away and had not been able to come before now and they are usually some of my first baby visitors. It seemed strange to have them come see my already two week old baby, Benjamin, instead of a newborn just hatched from the egg.

The hot summer sun was starting to wane as we opened our home delightedly to welcome them in that evening. Their arms were laden with the most awesome homemade food, gifts for Benjamin, snacks, and coffee break food for the evening. Laughter and talk bounced around in good jester as siblings reunited and tried to stay on top of the rivalry.

"Look at his long fingers!" remarked my youngest brother. "Get a basketball in those hands as soon as possible!"

"So much hair!" exclaimed one of my four sisters.

"I don't know who was happier you finally had a boy, you or me," declared one of my three brothers.

"I think he looks like Grandpa Mast," declared my older sister, Linda.

"Like you could tell who he looks like," my brother, Joe, just older than me scoffed in good-natured fun, "That's ridiculous. Every time we go visit a new baby, the women always do that. He/she looks just like so and so." He elevated his voice making it sound like a prissy girl. "You can't tell who a baby looks like when they're born. They just look like babies!" he insisted to the chagrin of his five sisters.

Joe ducked his head as a pillow was fired in his direction, narrowly missing its target as it bounced off the sofa behind him.

"Yep, they look just like babies," he repeated loudly, causing boisterous laughter to ring through the house.

"Well, this little baby is going to the doctor tomorrow for a well baby check. I don't usually do this, but something doesn't seem right. I will feel better knowing he is under a doctor's eye. Hey, Andrew," I exclaimed to my brother-in-law. I had suddenly remembered he was an EMT, and that maybe he could advise in some way. "Do you see anything that would be cause for alarm?" I asked, anxiousness crowding its way into my voice.

Andrew strolled over, carefully took Benny from me, and quietly observed him for a short while.

"You know, I want to say this as gently as possible and not to scare you. I'm not quite sure, but I think maybe he is breathing a little bit hard?" he answered cautiously. "I think it's a good idea to see the doctor. I see no need for a run to the emergency room, but definitely let a medical team check him out."

"Okay, thank you, Andrew. I will let you know if anything turns up," I answered, feeling an uneasy little crawly sensation of nervous energy begin to pile up inside of me. I knew. It was a beautiful and terrifying thing called a mother's intuition.

Behind the scenes, unknown to me, another pair of eyes saw. Mom eyes. The best kind of eyes there are. I learned later that Mom went home and cried on Dad's shoulder, voicing her fear that something was wrong with Benjamin. Mothers just know these things. My mom knows everything. She is sharper than the sharpest tack in the world. If you look up "sharp as a tack" in the dictionary, you will find my mom's name as the definition.

And so it came to pass, as the next warm July day dawned, I gathered my Benny and loaded him into the car along with Hannah. We then cruised to Salem where we would let the doctor have a look. I felt both apprehensive and hopeful as we pulled into the hot blacktop parking lot of the pediatrician's office. I looked forward to have an answer to the feeding issue. I was anxious to see what he weighed as I didn't have access to a baby scale. I walked inside to the over-packed waiting room and anticipated my turn.

FOUR

Your Baby Is Not Okay

"YOUR BABY IS NOT OKAY."

I couldn't breathe. The blood rushing through my ears was like water from a broken dam, pounding its way through my wildly beating heart and lungs at terrifying speeds. My world came crashing down like the twin towers at the severe impact from the massive jetliners. Where was God? Why would he do this to me? I wanted to cover my face with my quivering hands, tie my shoes, run away to hide from the doctor, or even get a root canal done. Anything would be better than to sit here, face to face, and be told this overwhelming news.

I must be brave and strong, I thought, making a strangling noise as the lump which was stuck in my throat refused to be swallowed. Whatever could possibly be wrong with our only son? I could hear the elderly lady doctor making clicking noises inside her cheek. They sounded like an annoying turn signal that had been forgotten. With trembling knees and wet tears running down my face, I immediately decided that I disliked her.

She had no chance, really. She was giving me bad news. It

31

wasn't totally her fault. Perhaps when the good Lord was handing out tact, she wasn't born yet, or maybe she was too busy to notice. All I know is that she didn't get a single drop as the gift got passed out. Not even one! Finally, after long, agonizing ticks and grunts, she formed actual words that I could understand.

"Mrs. Troyer, see, he has very large feet, yes, and notice his very, very long fingers, yes, and see how his thumbs remain firmly tucked inside his hands? He has ad-ducted thumbs, yes, and see his very long, narrow back?"

Yes doctor, I could see and notice. Especially when someone uses those two words so often it's beginning to sound like a tempo, slapping out the rhythm to a bad country song on the radio. Most assuredly I could see and notice.

"Does anyone in the family have a very long back?"

"Hmm, no, not excessively so," I sniffled and stammered.

"No? Well I think he has Marfan Syndrome," she announced firmly without any further information.

What on earth was Marfan Syndrome? I wanted papers in my hand with words and information. Did it mean that Benjamin would be mentally or physically disabled? That was certainly a description I thought I would never associate with one of my own dear children. I felt a groan coming from deep inside, protesting the thoughts that were racing through my troubled mind. *No! It could not happen to me.* How selfish is this thought, but we all think it, huh? If not me, then to whom *should* it happen?

So this is what it feels like to hear the doctor say something is wrong with your child, I thought brokenly to myself. I had similar thoughts when we had Sara. *So this is what it feels like to have a stillborn baby.*

"Oh!" screeched Dr. Tactless right into the miniscule ten by ten cubicle of an exam room.

A doctor should never exclaim so brazenly or so provokingly. As my startled brain settled back into my skull and my heart made the trip back down my throat, I realized she wasn't even making sounds inside her mouth. She had an alarmed aura about her that permeated the room, crawled up my spine, and caused sweat to roll down my body. Something was very wrong indeed.

"He has a heart murrrr-murrr!" she exclaimed in a thin, accusatory voice. I felt like the lowliest of Idaho Potatoes. One of those potatoes with so many eyes and roots that you end up throwing it away. That kind of lowly.

"Here, you listen," she said, handing me the stethoscope which was still warm from being in her ears. My brain was still quivering from being dislodged, so it didn't even register to be grossed out about her ear germs.

"Can you hear that extra wavy sound after each heartbeat?"

I nodded weakly. I could hear the additional rush after each precious beat. Not to mention the whooshing going through my entire being, leaving me with the strength of a bean.

"That extra whoosh means there is blood going places it shouldn't. Benjamin is likely going into heart failure as we speak. He must see a cardiologist right away."

I reached for Hannah's hand. Hannah was 6 years old and had come along to help carry the diaper bag. She had been my cheerful, chatty companion on the way in. I looked down at her. What could be going through her mind? I was terrified out of my wits. I was sure she would be traumatized for life and I already could picture the counselors lined up, giving her all manner of direction to sort through this moment of confusion in her young life. She looked back at me with her puppy brown eyes surrounded by auburn curls. There was a quiet, innocent trust in her gaze that told me she had confidence in me. I felt calmed and strengthened by her complete faith in a mother that was obviously not having a great day. *I must be brave!* I chided myself.

The itty bitty room became like a stuffed elevator as the doctor brought the other pediatricians from her team to confirm her suspicions. They weren't all agreed on Marfan Syndrome, but they were unified that we had some serious complications here. I had no idea what most of the conversation meant. It was a bunch of doctor lingo going back and forth from one person to another. I heard more abnormalities, like contracted joints, retracted jaw, concave chest, narrow shoulders, tight hips, hernias, and something with his eyes. They were having a medical science field day. I wanted to scoop Benjamin up and protect him from their prying eyes and pitying looks.

The next thing I knew, a red light was taped onto his foot. Tape. On his tender baby skin. It would surely hurt to take it off. What was it for, and why did they put it there? They started up a little monitor that brought up the number 87 and they panicked again.

"Mrs. Troyer, these SAT numbers are too low. A reading of 87 is much too low. You be sure to tell the cardiologist this number!"

We didn't even know what it meant.

"Okay. Yes, I will tell him." By this time my emotions were like a soggy noodle at best and I had no strength left to inquire what a "SAT" was. They kept mentioning it, so I knew it must be of great importance.

Nurses were coming at me from all directions, shapes and sizes, bringing appointment cards and a list of instructions and directions for amazing specialists located in big cities.

Did you know there is a doctor for every organ in the human body and that they all end with 'ologist'? Cardiologist... Gastroenterologist...Pulmonologist...on and on goes the list of 'ologists!'

Yes? Well, I didn't know that. I couldn't imagine visiting all these doctors or how we would ever afford them.

Being from the Amish, we had always taken personal responsibility for our own doctor bills. The close knit community I grew up in would host benefit auctions and events, drawing vast crowds to raise funds to pay doctor bills when they got very large.

"Oh, Lucy, be sure to tell Sherry to set up an appointment at the eye doctor. It is very likely Benjamin is blind!" the tactless pediatrician blurted into the chaos.

Hold everything! Please make the world stop turning. Did she say blind? But he looks right at us! The limp noodle inside of me had enough right then. I just stood there helplessly as hot tears rolled uncontrollably down my blotchy face. It was very embarrassing for me, but I couldn't quit crying. Even today I still cry and get hot and sweaty just thinking about that intense hour of my eventful life. I can honestly say it was the most overwhelming, heartbreaking sixty minutes I can remember. Despair hit me so deeply that all I could do was take one painful breath at a time. It hurt physically to inhale and exhale.

"Mrs. Troyer," Doctor Tactless gently touched my arm as she spoke. "I am so sorry. We have given you a lot today. I am so sorry."

I about fell over at the revelation that she had real honest-to-goodness feelings!

She was truly being compassionate, and gave me a quick hug while she continued, "Are you okay to drive him to the cardiologist or shall we call someone for you? They know you're coming, and will take great care of you."

Obviously, in my current sobby state, I appeared incapable of maneuvering a motorized vehicle.

"No, no, I will be fine," I managed to croak out between hiccuping sobs which still resonated from my size six shoes to the baseball stuck in my throat. *I must be brave! Help me to stop crying, please, Jesus!* I took a painful, deep breath, and forced the muscles surrounding my lips into a...smile? Ah, well, it was more like an unpleasant grimace than an actual smile, but I tried. Meanwhile she kept giving me the same directions over and over. Finally it sunk in that I would go right past our house, and I could stop and get Maynard. What a tremendous relief.

"So, Mrs. Troyer, you go straight through Salem..."

"I know how to get there," I snapped into the emotionally charged room. *I will use my highly evolved manners another time,* I thought, shocked at my own rudeness. I felt low class to snip at her like that, but at the same time, it made me feel a wee bit better. Like when you had just won a heroic battle against your fiercely competitive sibling.

"Oh, oh, yes, okay, you know the way," she murmured humbly in wide eyed amazement.

As Hannah handed me a fresh diaper, I gathered Benjamin's clothes and dressed him to quickly cover up all his little abnormalities (gulp) that they had so conspicuously pointed out. I loved him. I loved him so very much. More than when I had entered this despairing room. No matter that he was not okay; nothing could take away my love and commitment to my adorable son. I would care for him with every ounce of love inside of me.

I opened the door to go check out, and found dear nurse, Lucy, waiting in the hallway. Her arms were outstretched and big wallops of tears were running down her own cheeks. The kindness of her heart caused fresh scalding tears to overflow from my swollen eyes. We stood there for awhile as she softly encouraged me, and offered to walk with me to the car.

"Are you sure you should drive? I can call your husband, or get someone to take you to the hospital."

"Thank you, Lucy, but I'd rather go home, pick up my husband and we'll go together," I answered brokenly.

"Okay, if you're sure. Everything will be alright. The cardiologist office is absolutely wonderful. They are great at what they do, and will know exactly what Benjamin needs. He will get the best of care."

"Thank you, Lucy, thank you so very much. Goodbye."

She had no idea how much I appreciated her. To a soul suffocating with the pressure of hurt and despair, she was like a bright shining rainbow after a devastating storm. I know that God had put her in that tiny doctor's office that day for Hannah and me. My chest felt a little bit lighter as I walked down the hall toward the waiting room door. *Please God, let it be empty.* No curious starey-eyes to attach themselves to my puffy, red nose, rivaling a certain reindeer named Rudolph, please. I took a deep, painful, shaky breath, and turned the knob.

I looked up for only a moment, pausing mid-stride as it registered that the room was packed out to standing room only. *Oh, no!* I thought, agonizingly. What were they thinking as they noticed my tear streaked face, my swollen eyes, and the obvious sniffles that refused to be silenced? I wanted to tell them that my baby was not okay, that my world and my heart were crushed into bits and pieces and that I was scared right out of my skin. Instead, I kept placing one trembling foot in front of the other until I was outside in the bright summer sunshine.

I strapped Benjamin and Hannah into their car seats, and climbed into the driver's seat. I sat there for awhile, and blew the endless supply coming from my nose. As I put the van in reverse, and headed out of the parking lot, I gave the "great white beast", our old jalopy of a van, a cheer for doing as it was told. Foot on the gas...forward. Foot on the brake...slow down. Nice. It felt so normal and so right. I glared at people walking into Giant Eagle,

Wal-Mart and Aldi's, and realized that this good old U S of A would keep right on going. No matter what, the world keeps turning around and around, impatient to be getting on its rotating way around the sun. But my world had just been shattered.

It was a long 20 minute drive home. How would I tell Maynard that his little baby boy was not okay? How would I explain to Diana, 11, Laurie, ten, and Samantha, three, that their adored baby brother is not okay? What was that syndrome, starting with an M? I should have listened more closely and asked more detailed questions. What all did his heart condition involve? Would he ever be like other children? Was he blind? Blind? My mind couldn't process it all. Beeping alarms were going off, blaring warnings of an overload that could not be contained.

"Mom, why are you crying so much?" asked a troubled Hannah from the back seat.

"Hannah, dear," I said, "come up closer to Mom."

She let go of Benjamin's skinny hand, and leaned forward.

"Hannah, did you hear all those things the doctor said?"

"Yes, Mom, what did it mean?"

"Well, it means that there are things wrong on the inside of Benjamin, and Daddy and I are going to see the heart doctor as soon as we get back."

"Oh," she said thoughtfully, "I didn't like that doctor. She was a meaner. She shouldn't have said all those things about Benny, and made you cry so much."

My sweet girl! So like her to defend me. She is generally quiet, but when she opens her mouth it's usually profound.

I gave a weak smile at her choice of words for the doctor. A "meaner" was our family's personal language for mean people. I watched her lean back to Benjamin, give him a kiss and lean her head against his glossy black head of hair. *She will be his most fierce protector*, I thought to myself as we sped the last miles to home.

My thoughts trailed back to when I was pregnant with Benjamin. The intuition only a mother knows was in full swing, and we prayed every single day for a healthy baby. It felt like a desperate battle was going on inside of me that I couldn't see. After we had our Sara, I knew that a healthy baby was a divine miracle from heaven. Why did we have an unhealthy baby after so many prayers?

I was taken down a serious peg or two that day as the doctor had unceremoniously stripped me of any pride and pretense I may have carried regarding my amazing parental skills. Nothing could have prepared me for this day. I could not have known or understood had someone drawn up a blueprint.

As I automatically stepped on the brake and put on my left turn signal, my reverie was broken by the realization that we were at our driveway. *How did I get here so quickly? God help me be strong and brave as I tell Maynard. I don't handle drama well, Lord. Help me, please.*

FIVE

The Sun Sets on the First Day of Our New Life

"HANNAH, YOU STAY OUT here with Benjamin while I go get Daddy, then we'll take you and the other girls to Jon and Ellie," I said breathlessly. Dread washed over me as if it were the tide going out, taking everything along with it.

"Okay, Mom, I'll stay with Benny Boy, but hurry," she replied.

As I slowly walked to the house, I was glad no one came to greet me at the door.

I noticed the light switches right away, brightly covered with a paper that stated, "God is With Me."

It felt like eons ago, but it had only been that morning that Diana had been feeling artistic.

"Mom, may I print these light switch covers I found on the computer to color, and put them on all the switches? They say, 'God is With Me.' I will make them very beautiful!"

"Sure! I think that's a wonderful idea and it will be pretty," I answered with a smile.

Only God knew how much I needed this small word of encouragement this afternoon, I thought as I paused a moment to let it sink in.

"Oh, you're home..." Maynard came out of the kitchen and stopped mid-sentence when he saw my emotional puffy face. "Honey, what's wrong? Where are Benjamin and Hannah? Tell me!"

I ran into the safety of Maynard's arms and pointed out to the van as I burbled, "Something is wrong with Benjamin. We need to take him to the Cardiologist right away."

"What? Like what is wrong? Cardiologist? Does he have a heart condition? Honey, stop crying so you can talk," said Maynard as he took immediate charge. "Girls get in the van. I will call Ellie and arrange to drop them off."

I felt great relief. Everything would be okay. I could lean on Maynard now.

"So many things are wrong that I don't know where to start. She said he has a syndrome of some kind, and he might be blind!" I sobbed. A giant note of despair found its way into my voice box, and altered it as if I had just inhaled a hefty dose of helium.

After the girls were safely with our friend and neighbor, Ellie, Maynard reached for my hand.

"Now tell me what on earth is going on."

I did my best to explain everything. Our son would not be like other children. He had a syndrome starting with an M, a heart condition, hernias, possible blindness, and all the other devastating abnormalities. Maynard wanted more information, and could not fathom that so much could be wrong with Benjamin. Too exhausted to explain more, I drifted into silence the rest of the way, as he called friends to pray for us.

It only took 15 minutes to arrive at the plush office of the cardiologist.

Dr. Albram himself came out to greet us, "Hello, there! You must be the Troyers, and this must be Benjamin. I'm so happy to meet you. Oh, Benjamin is cute. Well, now, he looks okay. Dr. Tactless was all up in the air, but it doesn't look like an emergency. One of my nurses will be right out to get you, then we will get him all checked out and come up with a plan to maintain his heart murmur."

Dr. Albram could baby talk like a madman.

"Boo boo Benny ba ba where's Benny? There you are, boo boo boo!"

Had the situation not been so serious, I would have burst out laughing. He was insanely good at baby talk!

In order to retain some level of dignity, I restrained myself from kissing him smack dab in the face. He was a nice, old, wise man, who brought a ray of hope into an otherwise devastating day. He reminded me of my dear Grandpa Bontrager, who was one of the most awesome men in all of history. He spoke in the straight forward manner of my Grandpa, and had a kind face, a ready smile and a twinkle in his eye. The lively manner in which he spoke to Benjamin also mimicked Grandpa. I loved everything about him.

We waited only a few more minutes and then were escorted to the exam room by a kindly nurse. It felt strange and intimidating to be thrown into an unfamiliar medical world.

"Okay, sweet Benjamin, let's remove your clothes for an EKG," crooned the kindly nurse.

As I undressed him, I noticed her getting, oh no, stickers with wires on them. She was going to put all those on him? It seemed like there were enough to cover the whole state of Ohio! Sure enough, they were all stuck firmly onto his tiny chest.

The nurse made chit chat with us as she waited for the results of the EKG test.

"So how many children do you have?" she asked.

"We have four girls," answered Maynard.

"Four girls?" she gasped in shocked surprise, as if he had said her hair was on fire or that planet Mars had fallen and now there were little aliens running about. "You poor thing! Mr. Troyer, you wait until they're teenagers. You are in for a slippery ride on a steep downhill slope."

A fire lit in Maynard's eyes as he answered back quickly, "I'm blessed to have four girls. I am anything but poor because of them."

She laughed quietly and rolled her eyes. "I'm glad you think so!"

Next we were taken to a dimly lit room for an ultra sound of Benny's heart. It was quite interesting to see his heart pop up on the screen and watch it work. We are fearfully and wonderfully made.

As they carefully watched Benjamin's heart, we remained quiet in the hushed room. We heard Dr. Albram and the nurse exchange big words with meanings we didn't know or understand.

Finally Dr. Albram turned around to address us.

"Okay, Mom and Dad, what we have is an Atrial Septal Defect, which we call an ASD, and a Ventricular Septal Defect, which we call a VSD," the doctor said authoritatively and decisively. "This means Benjamin has two holes in his heart. He is under mild congestive heart failure right now, but we will get him on medication immediately, and it will keep it under control. This medication will try to make his heart work so hard that it will begin to form its own tissue to close those holes. We will give him ten months to a year, to see if they close by themselves. If indeed the medicine doesn't close them, we will re-evaluate the situation then. If he goes into heart failure before that, we will have to do emergency open heart surgery. We want Benjamin to weigh at least ten pounds before we do any surgery, though, but we will cross that bridge if we get there."

Open heart surgery? My breath was sucked out of me like coffee grounds being sucked by a vacuum. I put this bit of information far, far away on a shelf and decided to trust God and take one day at a time.

The doctor continued, "What we don't have is the heart condition that goes with Marfan Syndrome, so I have no reason to suggest he has it. Honestly, I don't think he does. And, now, Dad, you take Mom home and get her some rest. She has had a very long day." He smiled kindly and wished us the best and that he would see us back the next day to check up on things.

Then he turned around and added, "If you are worried about paying, you can relax. Because Benjamin was born with these heart defects he is automatically approved for BCMH. That stands for Bureau for Children with Medical Handicaps. Okay, Mom and Dad and Benny Boy, we will see you again soon. Bye Benny boo boo boo boy. Benny! Where's Benny? Boo!" He baby talked, smiled broadly, and waved as he cheerily waltzed out the door.

I loved him so much. He had handed us a lifeline and he didn't even know it. BCMH? I vaguely remember hearing of it before. Somewhere in Holmes County, Ohio, they have benefit auctions for this fund, I think. Whoever would have thought that we would one day be a very humble recipient of this generous program?

So once again, we dressed our little not-okay baby and tucked him into the car seat with grateful hearts to be taking him home after so much uncertainty.

We stopped at the pharmacy to pick up Benny's medications. The pharmacist read the medication and got a knowing look.

"Is this the baby receiving these meds?" he asked kindly.

"Yes, this is Benjamin." we answered apprehensively.

"Well, I want you to know he will do great once he's on this medication. My daughter had the exact same heart condition, and this medication and a whole lot of prayers allowed her to avoid surgery altogether. I will pray for Benjamin that the same thing will happen to him," he stated faithfully.

"Thank you so much for your prayers!" we said as we smiled through our tears and headed out to the car.

It was these little things that kept us going that first bewildering day on our new journey. God has a way of placing encouraging people in our paths when we are on a difficult trail.

We stopped at Jon and Ellie's house to pick up the girls.

Ellie came rushing out anxiously. "Is Benny Boy okay? What happened? What can we do to help? The girls have all had their baths and I fed them a good supper. I saved some for you if you would like some?"

"Benny is not okay, but we have medications to help. Come over for coffee tomorrow morning and I will fill you in. Thank you so much for taking care of the girls for us. And we would love those plates you fixed. You're an angel!" We quickly exchanged a few more words and loaded up the girls and headed home.

We arrived home, and I collapsed on the couch, clutching my dear son as close as possible, only letting him go when Diana and Laurie needed to hold him close to their budding mother hearts as well. We were all in this together, and we were all smitten by Benny Love Disease.

No sooner did we get home than a familiar green van pulled up to our driveway.

I heard the girls let out a yelp of glee.

"Mom, Eddie Millers are here! Should I quickly make some coffee?" asked Diana, ever the responsible one who took charge as only the oldest in the family does.

"Oh, I'm so glad they're here! Sure, go ahead and start a pot of coffee." *I hope I can hold it together while they're here*, I mused, giving myself a quick talking-to. *You have cried enough, so hold it in, girl.*

I didn't do too well with holding back, but they are dear friends that we have known for a long time. They stopped in to encourage us, and they cried alongside us as they wrapped their arms around us. It meant so much. We didn't know what our future held, but we had wonderful friends and family. I remember so well their strapping young son firmly stating, "I don't believe a word that doctor said. There is nothing wrong with Benjamin. He does not have a syndrome!"

It brought a smile to my face and a tear to my eye at his protective heart towards Benny and us.

They drank a cup of coffee with us, and prayed with us before they said goodbye.

After they left I thought about the word *syndrome*. What did it mean to me? The word syndrome was something I associated with people that were not "normal". When I was a little girl it meant the children that rode on the Happy Hill School Bus. The short bus. The small bus was only for children a little bit loose in the head. When I was a wee lass, these children made me feel uncomfortable. They made the hair on my arms rise, yet I was fascinated by them and I couldn't look away. Okay, I stared.

It would be the worst nightmare in the world to have a child on that bus, I used to think.

As siblings, we would pick on each other about belonging on the Happy Hill bus. And secretly, inside the innermost and insecure spot of my maturing young heart, I wondered if, indeed, *maybe I should be on that small yellow school bus*. Maybe there was something wrong with me and I didn't realize it. There. Now I have shared a deep, dark, terrible lie that I believed about myself for a long time.

The good news is that Jesus heals the broken-hearted and sets the captives free. I was one of those shattered prisoners of my own fears and now I am gloriously set free!

I used to feel offbeat when my healthy children got sick, with a few sniffles here and there, or when they ran a low-grade fever. I was unable to rest and relax until everything was back to normal.

Now our new normal would be to live every single day with the knowledge that not all was okay. We were suddenly being required to live this way all the time, and it felt impossible.

Fortunately for us, impossible is not in God's vocabulary! Possible is. For with God, all things are possible. What a blessed people we are to have this precious promise!

SIX

Diagnostics for Days

THE FOLLOWING DAYS were filled with endless doctor appointments and diagnostics. We paraded Benny in front of many physicians, for many organs, in all shapes, sizes and manners.

One particular doctor stands out in my memory. A single time in the presence of this one was enough to last a lifetime. He was like a mangy grizzly bear coming out of hibernation. Well, this guy was supposed to examine my darling baby boy for hernias. I was terrified the minute I set eyes on him! I was even more alarmed when he ripped open Benny's diaper and poked, yanked and prodded at his very private parts. I'm pretty sure *I* resembled a mama bear with furry cubs, if he had bothered to look.

All of a sudden he bellowed, "These aren't hernias! These are his testicles! Now get out of here. We never need to see you again!"

We got out of there quickly. Months later we found out Benjamin did indeed have hernias and needed surgery to repair them.

Life went on and we settled into a new normal. Benjamin was loved and adored by his four sisters and got all the attention in the world.

Mom, otherwise known as myself, was a disaster. That is all. There are no other words to describe it. I knew something was still not right. Despite being on heart medication and the calorie laden milk enhancer packets that were dumped into each bottle, Benjamin would not gain weight. No matter what I did, he would not nurse, and he barely took a bottle.

Twice we took Benjamin to the emergency room because I was just sure something else was wrong. Twice we got sent home with the same diagnosis. He was underweight and delayed because of his heart condition. We were instructed to keep doing what we were doing and give him time to catch up.

I was thankful for the weekly doctor appointment Benny and I were required to keep. Every seven days, I took Benjamin in, so they could weigh him and see how he was doing. On one particular visit Dr. Tactless sat me down and told me in no uncertain terms, "Mrs. Troyer, you must get him to eat. If he won't eat for you, he will need to be taken off breast milk and breast milk enhancer and put on a high calorie milk formula. He is almost three months old, and still not putting on any pounds."

"But that's just it!" I pleaded desperately. "I can't get him to drink even a bottle! I have been pumping my own milk all these weeks, and have been adding the extra calorie packets to it, but he drinks very little. He is always sweaty from trying. In fact, we strip him down to his diaper because he perspires so badly when he tries to eat. Literally, Dr. Tactless, he is dripping wet from head to toe. Is this okay? Also, I have noticed that so much of what he does try to take, runs out both sides of his mouth!"

"Mrs. Troyer, I repeat, you must make him eat. The sweating comes from his heart condition. This is a normal symptom of a heart disease. Drinking a bottle is like running a marathon for him because his heart is working so hard. You have to be patient and give him enough time to get all those ounces down. Don't give up!"

I looked at her. This made no sense at all. The light and spark that normally resonated from my calm, happy demeanor was nowhere to be found. I was like a sad, deflated balloon lying defeated on the cold hard ground with no hopes of ever being revived again.

"But...should it take two hours for him to drink two ounces?" I asked incredulously.

She shook her head at me. "Patience, Mrs. Troyer, patience and perseverance. I will give you one more week. If he hasn't gained any weight in that time we will put him on a high calorie formula. Okay, that is all for today, I will see you soon and hope for better results."

I was so distraught at her pitiful attempt to help that I went home and wept huge sobbing rivers of tears for my son. My heart was in anguish. Why would he not gain weight? Why did milk run out the sides of his mouth? Why did it take him hours to swallow just 2 ounces of milk? Why was he drenched in sweat from head to skinny toe when he tried to drink a bottle? Why, at almost three months of age was he not even trying to conquer head control? Why, why, why?

All my frustrations and unanswered questions were fired upon my ever kind and very tolerant husband. One day, he just had enough. His vast stash of patience, (and he has storehouses full of it), dried up altogether right then and there. The last straw broke the camel's back.

"Honey, there is nothing wrong with Benjamin. He has a heart condition and this makes him slower and delayed from other babies. Even the doctors at the emergency room keep telling us this. I am sick of hearing it. Now stop it! You run to the doctor for every little thing. I think Benny is fine. He'll just have to catch up."

Oh I was super duper mad at him that day! I was furiously thinking up all manner of retaliation and revenge for what he said! Me? A doctor chaser?! Never! But in that same moment, the fight inside of me died because I so desperately wanted to believe that what he said was true. I concluded that I would not worry any more. If Benny was hungry, he would eat. Until then he would be smothered with love and kisses and the best care ever. I found myself in survival mode, and barely pulling through one miserable day after another.

In our 12 years of married life, we had hardly ever fought or argued. Well, let me tell you something shocking. Having a special needs child sapped the tar out of all we thought we had or knew! And we had ourselves some real earth-rocking fights and arguments! We look back now and understand that our world was an emotional firecracker just waiting for a spark to set it off. But it works the other way, too, and sometimes when we had just said something especially nasty we would begin to laugh until we cried because it was so obnoxious. We knew we never meant such awful things.

It was October 31, 2003. Benjamin was almost four months old. He had not slept for two days and fretted constantly. By this time, his appointments with Dr. Tactless had been scheduled out in two-week intervals. He had gained a few ounces and had been cleared as being delayed but gaining. But the feeding issues had gotten worse. Much worse.

"Maynard, can you see how Benjamin breathes when sucking on his bottle? He sucks and gets a mouthful of milk, then kind of makes a strangling noise like he is trying to catch his breath. Basically, all of the milk runs out of the sides of his mouth. I can't take it anymore. I want him to see a doctor now."

I was a little afraid to broach this delicate subject to Maynard. I did so very cautiously and with an airplane load of tact.

Maynard agreed that I should take him to see the doctor.

Dr. Tactless was out of town so she had a substitute there in her place.

I liked this new doctor immediately. I could see concern, compassion and care in her eyes towards Benjamin.

"See on Benjamin's chest area here, how he is retracting?" she asked gently.

"Uh, what's that mean?" I asked. We were completely ignorant of anything medical.

"Sure, I will explain. See how when he breathes, he sucks in his skin around the bones of his chest. See also how his nostrils are flaring? These are all signs of respiratory distress, meaning he is struggling for every breath he takes. Something is not quite right. Let's give him an albuteral treatment to see if it will make a difference."

The doctor stuck her head out into the hall and asked quietly for Lucy, then instructed her to set up the nebulizer for Benny.

"So, I am also very concerned about his weight. Let's see, he is almost four months old and weighs little more than six pounds? What was his birth weight again?" she asked as she nimbly flicked through his chart. She scanned until she found it. "Oh! He was almost six pounds at birth? What has Dr. Tactless been doing?" I could hear the alarm in her voice.

"We have been trying so hard to get his weight up," I replied. Tears were starting to crowd my throat.

"Don't worry, Mrs. Troyer. I will help you," she smiled assuredly.

This may sound a little strange, but I felt like jumping up and down. Someone was actually helping us? Respiratory distress was never good, but I was so happy to let her carry my load for just a moment, that I wasn't even alarmed.

If she had said, "Mrs. Troyer, the only way I will help you is if you eat this entire bag of slimy okra," I would have inhaled that horrible item they call food right on the spot. I may or may not have even eaten the plastic bag!

The nebulizer whirred quietly as the mist carried across Benjamin's sweet face.

After a few minutes of treatment, the doctor said, "Mrs. Troyer, this albuteral treatment is not helping. There is no change in his retractions, and his nostrils are still flaring. His SAT levels are at 89. We need to get him to an emergency room immediately. He may have some kind of obstruction in his windpipe area." She immediately set things into action to have us ordered into the emergency room.

The parachute I had been blissfully gliding on collapsed and dropped me with a thud on the hard-packed road of reality. *Here I am again, Lord, hearing these awful things about my Benny. No! Would it never end?*

"Alright, then what do I need to do?" I was surprised at the strength in my voice. I was getting good at this. I looked down on the floor just to make sure I wasn't lying there in a puddle of tears. Nope. I was standing on my own two feet, ready to march on to the next phase.

"Take him to the nearest children's hospital instead of the local emergency room. You will get much better care there. Are you okay? I am so sorry, but we need to get help for him right away."

Was I okay? Of course not, but someone was helping me. Finally.

I walked weakly out to the great white beast otherwise known as our van. What a precious baby I held in my arms! I held him closely a few minutes longer before handing him to Laurie. She immediately rained upon him with sweet love and a hearty dose of wet kisses.

"I love you, Benny," she crooned as tears slid down her cheeks, "you are the cutest and the sweetest. Mmm."

I watched for a minute. If only he could gain weight on hugs, kisses and love. If so, we would have to put him on a diet, he would be so pudgy and fat we couldn't carry him.

Laurie climbed in and cuddled Benny on her lap. He couldn't sit in his car seat, because he couldn't breathe in that tilted position! I look back and shake my head, and my heart drops to new lows. Why didn't we insist that the doctors take a better look? I cannot allow myself to go back, but I must thank God for what I have today, and the great blessing we have in having such an amazing person as Benny in our lives.

I dropped Laurie off at Jon and Ellie's house where the other children had stayed while we had gone to the doctor. Maynard met me there, and we took Benjamin to the emergency room quickly.

The nurse at the triage desk took him, and was about to take his weight, etc, when she whirled around and said in a shocked voice, "How long has this baby been like this?" She stared in shock at the skinny mass of tiny human form we called Benny. She didn't even bother with vitals as she nodded to the second equally disturbed nurse, "I'm taking him back right away!"

Um, excuse me? I almost burst a blood vein from the extreme adrenalin rush of intense outrage that wanted to explode into the suddenly terribly warm triage room. Was I hearing right? It sounded suspiciously like she was accusing us of something. It was a low blow and terribly hard for me to swallow the colossal pill being shoved down into my gullet. It made me furious. Like I hadn't been trying to tell his doctor that I cannot make him eat. This was his third emergency room visit to this very same hospital where we had tried to get help, and each time we got sent home.

She didn't wait to give us a chance to respond as she whisked Benjamin down the hall yelling, "We need a cardiac team right now! Respiratory! Nurse! Doctor!"

The exam room was small and there was no room for Maynard and me. We stood helplessly outside and watched as the team worked quickly to hook up tiny little Benny to IV's and all manner of machinery. There was a lot of tape attached to his tender baby skin, and a mask on his face. Hospitals thrive on tape and masks no matter how tiny or tender the skin. We had so much to learn.

When the dust settled and we were grandly escorted to our PICU room by the green pajama clad gentleman, we still didn't have any answers. Nobody really knew what could be wrong.

I was terrified they would send us home without answers and I voiced my fears to our nurse.

"Mrs. Troyer, this baby will not go anywhere unless he gains about ten pounds first. It will take time, but we will get to the bottom of his failure to thrive." She kindly squeezed my hand and added, "Do not worry. We will figure it out."

Thus began our hospital life. To this day we never know what lies in front of us from one day to the next. We only know that God promised his grace would be sufficient. Does he give us more than we can take?

"Well, you know, God never gives you more than you can handle," good intentioned people say in their infinite wisdom, walking away, clearing their throat like they had just presented us with the divine answer to all our impossible issues.

How about this line, "Did you know that Tristan has cancer? THAT would be a hard situation." True. That would be very difficult.

What they are trying to communicate is words of comfort. But what we hear is, "This shouldn't hurt. You shouldn't cry over something as small as this. Someone else has it much harder. Did you hear that Becky has two broken legs? You only have one broken leg. So yours shouldn't hurt at all."

No matter what people are going through, there is always someone else who has it much worse, but it doesn't mean we should tell them this in a way so that it makes them feel like their own hurts are minimal. It is not encouraging to someone who is going through a bewildering time in life when circumstances don't make any sense, and it feels pretty much like they have more than they can bear.

When I hear the line, "You can just be thankful; because so and so just found out they have …." I feel a sudden urge to make a rapid exit in the opposite direction. Instead, tell me that God loves me, that He understands we are carrying a huge load. Remind me that He knows how bad we are hurting, and that He promises to never leave. Assure me that he will sometimes have to carry us, and that most of all He will make his grace sufficient, even when we don't understand.

I have run to my bedroom many times throughout the years and wailed at God to please make his grace adequate for a very intensely extreme moment. At my lowest points, in my darkest hours, His light shines through for me and I can receive His grace! He has never failed to meet my needs, even while giving me more than I can endure.

Back to the hospital!

After two days in PICU they released us to the regular floor, where the nurses run flat out constantly and are not right outside your door like in the intensive care unit. Floor nurses are completely over-worked. I only hope they are not under-paid, because they are fantastic and try very hard to reach around to their multitude of patients.

We still did not have any answers at all, except maybe a minor pneumonia.

Our room on the normal floor was so small it was almost invisible. There was only room for our teeny, tiny, orange-gowned Benjamin in a full sized hospital bed. He looked like a pea on a king-sized mattress. An orange pea. Then there was the ridiculous cot where Maynard and I both squeezed to sleep at night. We desperately held on to each other in our pain. The first night we had just settled down when the door burst open with a vengeance! In strode the over-sized night nurse. Groan! It's very humbling to have someone gawking at your two bodies trying not to slide off a weensy cot. Ultimate awkwardness! She came barreling in, pushing her little blood pressure pole thing, crashing into us, the unsuspecting wall, and anything else in her innocent pathway.

"Good grief. It's a baby elephant," Maynard snickered into my ear. Of course we got the giggles; we huffed, sputtered, held our breath, and about wet ourselves to keep from totally busting out in hilarious guffaws of belly laughs!

There was no laughter the next day. Benjamin had gotten worse overnight, and had trouble breathing. His nurse, Lily, worked hard all day to keep up to his needs plus all the other patients in her care. Before she left her long, exhausting shift, she called the young, tall, darkly handsome doctor in, and tried to educate him on the fragile condition Benjamin was in.

"I am not comfortable with his labored breathing. He needs to be in PICU," she explained, quietly speaking her opinion as she apprehensively awaited his response.

The young doctor swooped up Benjamin to cuddle him in his arms, while he tenderly crooned, "Oh, he's so cute and he smells so good, hmm. You know, I think he's fine. Does he have major issues? Yes. But I am comfortable keeping him on the floor for the night. We will reevaluate the situation in the morning."

I watched the nurse uneasily. She was clearly upset, but refrained from further comments.

Bright and early the next morning, Lily popped in, ready to embrace another day of hard work.

"What are you guys still doing here? I told them under no uncertain terms that you would be in PICU when I come in today." Indeed, because we were not in PICU, she exploded. I checked for a fire extinguisher to fan the flames shooting straight from the dark eyeballs of Lily. She was like a bomb ready to go boom. She glanced frantically at Jon, the respiratory therapist who had labored with Benny all night. "Jon! Help me out here!"

Jon rolled his eyes in exasperation. "I have been giving him breathing treatments all night long. They are not helping at all. I told the doctors this, and that I believe we have obstruction in his throat area, but they won't listen to me! I am getting very upset at them."

Rounding up a roomful of harried doctors and concerned respiratory therapists she ranted, raved and scolded them all to shame.

"Now, listen. I was here yesterday, and this baby is very sick. He will quit breathing if someone doesn't do something. He is not a floor patient and he must be in PICU where there is a team to help him if he does his fake breathing! He needs a twenty-four hour nurse. I cannot give him the care he needs and I will not have this. I mean just look at him! He will quit if you don't do something!" she raved again.

She glanced at me, noticing for the first time that I was weeping non-stop.

"Oh, no, Mrs. Troyer, it's going to be okay. It will be alright, truly, please believe me. We will help Benny! He will be fine. We just need to get him to PICU where he will have a nurse at his side at all times." She came over and gave me a quick hug. I was not comforted.

"This is not good," I overheard one doctor say. "He definitely needs to be in PICU, and should probably be transferred to Rainbow."

So we made the trek back to PICU with weary, downcast hearts. We were not there more than a half hour when the doctor on duty strolled in saying, "We need to transfer Benjamin to a bigger hospital, and we think Rainbow Babies of Cleveland Ohio will be our best option."

He explained the possibility of some kind of obstruction going on in his windpipe area, and assured us they had a great team of doctors that were highly trained for these circumstances. Within an hour the team from Cleveland was there to transport Benny, and we were on our way.

We noticed the difference in the professional manner in which they handled Benjamin right away. Even the amazing PICU nurses had seemed intimidated by their presence. We felt confident that we were in good hands.

And so we made the journey to Rainbow Babies in Cleveland, Ohio. As I rode in front with the ambulance driver, I noticed the immense buildings surrounding us as we entered Cleveland, and it felt like we were in the largest city on the planet. Apprehension and fear wanted to crawl their way up my leg and take up permanent residence in my heart. I glanced back through the opening at Benny riding quietly on the gurney. He was covered in a cozy blanket, his shiny mop of black hair the only color popping out.

The EMT noticed me and smiled kindly. He moved up to the window in the ambulance gently saying, "Benny is doing great. He had one breathing episode, but he is fine again. We are almost there, and he will be in the best hands he could possibly be. You will be so happy you transferred to this hospital."

Maynard had followed the ambulance in our 1992 clunky van. As he pulled into the parking garage, the old van protested with a loud bang. Just like that. Park. Bang. *It feels just like we do*, I thought. I felt like parking myself, making a loud, howling bellow, and refuse to believe that this was me, on this trail of overwhelming despair of not knowing what on earth was wrong with Benny. Was he truly a special needs child? Surely not! I felt like I couldn't handle having a special needs child. How would we ever survive it if he was? We would forever be that spectacle of a family, rolling into town in the great white beast, as people lined up to stare.

Then I heard it, the still small voice of God, "Cast all your cares on me, I will help carry your burdens and fears. I created Benjamin. Isn't he so sweet? Won't you love him even if he is a special needs child, never to be as other children?"

He got my full attention. Of course we would love our Benny no matter what. Adoring Benny would not be an issue. I was hopelessly smitten with the love of a mother that would not go away no matter what. It was settled in my heart to dedicate myself to him, whatever it took. I was so thankful for the mother-love that God has given me. It truly was a gift.

SEVEN
Rainbow Babies Hospital

"DON'T TRY GETTING into the hospital this way," smiled the kind transport guy as he took us in through the Rainbow Babies basement, and down long, spotless hallways, around a zillion corners, and finally onto an immaculate elevator. It was evening and we had just arrived. Doctors and nurses were everywhere as we stepped with trepidation through the double doors of the brightly lit intensive care unit. The air seemed to have an aura of professionalism, while at the same time it felt immense and cold. A team of doctors and nurses immediately surrounded us and took charge of Benjamin.

Our nurse, Ashley, smiled a lot. We loved her immediately. She adored Benny, and quickly decided he needed one of the newer cribs.

"Ralph, I need one of the new soft cribs. This little bear cub deserves to be as comfortable as can be. There's an extra one in room 21, so go get it quickly before someone beats you to it!" She winked at us, making us feel like we were getting the best care, and that the President of the United States wouldn't have been treated any more like royalty than Mr. Ben.

Ashley kept a keen eye on Benny, rarely stepping out of the room. She immediately observed his fake breathing. It escalated soon after we got there. We stood by his side constantly watching for it, and then gently shaking him to make him take an actual breath. He would pretend to breathe, moving his chest up and down, without actually moving any air into his lungs. It was terrifying to us, and very unnerving to Ashley, who kept the "button" close at hand at all times to call for help.

"Let's try bi-pap and see if he responds," the house doctor asserted authoritatively, sending his peers about fetching this and that as they were instructed.

The doctor turned around to address us. He spoke with a concerned edge to his voice, "So for now, the plan is to see if the bi-pap will keep him from fake breathing. We don't yet understand why he is doing this. Unfortunately, we can't have him doing it, or one of these times he won't recover from it. He is wearing out, and he will just quit trying soon. He is frail and weak to begin with. He needs to direct all his energy towards getting well. Right now, in the short time that I have seen him, I can say that his energy is all going for the next struggling breath. Please be aware that the next step will be a ventilator, which will do all the breathing for him, so that his body can rest and heal."

We nodded our understanding and consent, watching as the amazing team of medical personnel worked on Benny like he was the only person in the whole hospital. We felt terrified, but blessed.

"How long was he at the other hospital?" continued the doctor.

"We were there for four days," we answered.

"Hmm." He shook his head. "That's too bad. He needed better care long before this. I want you to understand that this is very serious. Benjamin is in bad shape."

We remained silent, and looked at him helplessly. We wished we would have done things differently, but that was no longer an option.

I had stepped out of the room to use the restroom and came back to a ferocious Benjamin. He was screaming as loud as a teeny little boy in his fading condition could at the ridiculous contraption strapped onto his face. He fought that bi-pap until he was completely exhausted. Only he didn't stop there. He kept right on going.

"Oh, my goodness, get that thing off him!" I yelped into the stressed out room.

All heads swiveled in my direction like puppets controlled by a string, at my rather loud outburst. I'm sure they were in wonder and awe at the little lady who thought she had an actual chance at telling them what to do. I had just about had enough, and it looked like my Benny did as well.

"You are right, Mom. This will not do. We must sedate him and put him on the vent. We would rather be safe than sorry. With your permission, we will get the vent orders started right away. Benjamin's will to survive is as big as Texas, and he will not stop fighting that Bi-pap until it's too late. I am so sorry to have to do this, but in my professional opinion, it's the only way he will survive for now."

"Yes, okay, whatever is best for Benjamin," we answered tiredly.

We were too exhausted to be capable of thinking straight. In fact, we were so bone-weary, that when they chased us out of the room to insert a breathing tube, we went out to the lobby and lay flat on the seats. Never mind politely sitting and delicately tilting our heads for rest. Our sense of properness and dignity were all gone far, far away to a land where only correct people remain. We prostrated ourselves in horizontal positions with nary a blanket or pillow and closed our eyes. What did people think? Three words, *we don't care!* We were out of gas, and our baby was not okay.

"Maynard, wake up!" I exclaimed in shock an hour later, as I wiped the drool off the seat of the lounge bench I had been snoozing on. "A whole hour has gone by. They must have forgotten about us."

"Wha...are you kidding me? That makes me so upset. They said in a worst case scenario, it would take 45 minutes. C'mon, let's go back in," Maynard said in dismay.

Still shaking off the slumber wanting to zone in on us, we marched up to the "guard" stationed at the PICU doors. We showed off our shiny paper badges that were pinned to our bodice, and announced us as parents to a child in PICU, and he opened the doors without hesitation.

We made it about ten feet inside the double whammy doors when we were halted in our tracks by the doctor himself.

"Mindy, how did they get in here?" The resident doctor came running, looking a tad bit harried. "Mr. and Mrs. Troyer, I am so sorry. We are having trouble inserting the tube. Normally it doesn't take long, but Benjamin's airway is wiggly and floppy. Elnora is with him now. She is the best of the best, and it will not be much longer, I promise. Please, wait outside and we will come get you the minute he is settled. Get them a buzzer, Mindy, so we can buzz them as soon as we are ready."

We took the buzzer, attached it to Maynard's belt, and turned around with a worried glance at all the medical personnel surrounding Benny's doorway at room number four.

It felt like we were characters in a story. Oh, how I longed to quickly skip back to the last chapter, a trait of mine, to read the ending! Would the baby end up okay? Surely they would find a medicine and the baby would snap completely out of it and be well. Would the parents end up fighting like banshees? Would their marriage survive the vicious onslaught of their new requirements of living? What would happen to their precious girls at home? But, alas, I had no choice but to keep "reading" where I was. No sneak peeks are allowed in the real world.

To pass the time, we wandered around the halls, and familiarized ourselves with our surroundings, and waited for the buzzer they gave us to go off. We found a beautiful, refreshing atrium with real life sized trees growing right there, inside the building. There were impressive gift shops, a library, and a cafeteria that was said to be great. But at that hour in the night all we could smell or purchase was old, stale pizza.

"Am I eating cardboard or pizza? Is this cheese or a hair? Oh, yeah, it's cheese. Too stringy for hair." muttered Maynard under his breath, as we burst out in tense giggles. "Oh! It's time to go back. The buzzer just went off!" We hurriedly disposed of our empty pizza plates.

It had been two hours since we had been ushered out of the unit. We entered Benjamin's room uneasily, not knowing what we would find. Benjamin was hooked onto the ventilator plus a ton of other machines and gadgets. We didn't know what they all were, but we asked many questions, and received a free education with a capital "E". It was a great relief to see Benjamin relaxed and completely sedated. His slight chest rose and fell rhythmically to the pattern of the settings on the machines. His tired little body finally could rest while everyone tried to figure out what was going on inside of him.

At this moment the paperwork began in earnest. It seemed we plowed through an intense amount of endless inquiries.

The doctor addressed us with a barrage of questions. "Mrs. Troyer, does he aspirate?"

Really? As if I know what that word means! It sounds like some-

thing awful. Choked? I hemmed and hawed while I scrambled frantically about in my fatigued brain for a definition to such a word as aspirate.

It was one question too many so I did the most composed thing on earth. Right there in front of the highly impressive doctor I burst into exhausted tears. Then in a voice as tiny as a mustard seed I continued between hiccuping sobs, "I don't know what aspirate means and I don't know if he aspirates."

The phrase, *what does that mean*, became my second nature. I learned to ask it loudly and boldly and without shame. I asked it all the time and every day until I finally had my medical act together and understood the terminologies associated with Benny's condition.

The doctor looked at me, then at Maynard, silently asking him what is wrong with his blubbering wife as she quickly explained the definition of aspirate.

"Honey, why are you crying?" urged Maynard in bewilderment.

"I don't know!" I gulped, crying even harder.

"You know what? It's okay." The doctor stepped in, and rescued me from melting like a snowman on the beaches of Florida. "You have had a long day. We will do the rest tomorrow. You sleep the best you can. This couch pulls out into a small bed and there are extra blankets and pillows in this closet. We just had a young couple that slept together in it for three months, so you should be comfortable. I will see you in the morning."

Finally our nightmare of a day is coming to an end, I thought as we pulled the privacy curtain around the tiny bed.

We didn't know that a hospital never sleeps. It's like New York City, where the lights never go out, sirens and alarms go off at any given moment, and voices are always within hearing. It never gives living, breathing souls a moment of quiet.

66

I woke up with a jolt, sensing that a whole crowd of doctors and nurses were surrounding Benjamin. Whipping back the curtain I stepped out to see what was happening.

"We are trying to insert a femoral line. It's a line we take through the groin, straight into his heart. It isn't working for us, so we will leave it for the moment. You can go back to sleep," the doctor assured me, willing this mother hen to stop minding their business, which actually was my business. Benny was on the top of my list of things to keep my nose poked into, and no one was going to stop me.

The ventilator was a honking, whining, whistling monster, carrying on all night long. It nearly drove us crazy that first night. The P.A. System loudly proclaiming,

"Respiratory to room #4. Respiratory to room #4, please."

Then the frustrated respiratory humans came to try, try, and try to fix the "leak", all to no avail. The next morning the nurses rejoiced at the arrival of a certain respiratory therapist because he was the only one who really understood how to make this state of the art monster stay quiet. Today, 14 years later, I can still hear the sound patterns of the ventilator alarms whining like a kid being denied a bright, red lollipop, in a candy store.

Test after test were performed. They were tests with big words mostly ending with "scope" or "scopy". This meant that cameras or instruments were sent to various parts on the inside of Benjamin to give the doctors a visual eye as to what could be keeping him from thriving. Everything turned up negative. Seven long days turned into weeks with no answers or progress. Our stay at Rainbow Babies became a turbulent storm like never before.

Before the girls came for the first time, the counselors took pictures of Benny hooked up to his machines. His tiny body was barely visible through a myriad of tape and tubing.

"Okay, girls, come with me," smiled Tracy sweetly. "I want to show you a picture of Benny before you go in to see him. See all this tape and tubing? It's all there to keep him safe. He is not in any pain, and he will sleep the whole time you see him because we gave him medicine so he can rest. You understand?"

The girls nodded their heads.

"Okay, sweethearts, let's go visit Benny!"

I watched as they cautiously walked in and saw the shock that went over their precious faces when their eyes fell on Benny. Diana's lips began to quiver and big whoppers of tears ran down her cheeks. Laurie soon joined and they both sobbed quietly as we, along with Tracy, assured them it was okay to be sad and cry. Hannah and Samantha were too young to fully grasp the situation, but because everyone else cried, they did as well.

"Hannah and Samantha would you like a Popsicle?" asked Tracy.

"Yes!" Hannah and Samantha spoke eagerly in unison.

"Come with me then!" laughed Tracy.

This started a Popsicle marathon unparalleled to any that hospital has ever seen. The girls received multiple Popsicles every single time they came, much to their delight. Every nurse wanted to be the one earning the approval of our little princesses, so whenever a new shift started, guess what? Popsicles!

As the days went on, Maynard and I clung to each other, because the discouragement and despair wanted to wash us down the river. We shed many tears of pain, exhaustion, fear, helplessness and longing for normal. We even got mad at each other and spoke in snarly voices.

One day we had ventured out of the hospital for the first time to purchase an everyday essential. Upon returning, for some reason we could not find the parking garage.

"Maynard, this is not the right parking lot. You are so ridiculous!" I exclaimed in real disgust as he pulled into the tiniest hospital parking lot I had ever seen. "This must be a doctors' parking lot. I bet we aren't even allowed to be in here!"

"Yes, we are. Otherwise it would be gated with only a doctor's pass allowing us to enter. Look, there is what looks like the main entrance." he snorted back with just as much vehemence as I had dished out.

"What? Are you kidding me? I've seen many hospital entrances and this cannot be one, it's much too small!" I could hear my ugly, snarky tone and hated it, but I couldn't seem to stop myself.

"We are parking right here, right now," replied Maynard determinedly. I, for sure, didn't like my tone, but his tone was as black as thunder.

We got out and walked up to the door, but lo, it was not a hospital entrance at all. We sauntered over to the park-like area nearby and looked for someone to steer us in the right direction.

"Hello, ma'am, could you tell us where the main entrance to the hospital is?" Maynard asked patiently.

As she turned I noticed that her bright blue shirt and her too short, orange pant legs were not the most smartly dressed wardrobe I had ever seen, especially considering the snow white socks boldly proclaiming their presence firmly held in place by none other than flip flops. I don't trust anyone who wears socks with flip flops. Neither do I trust people who take pictures of their breakfast of dippy eggs. Who takes pictures of eggs? That's just gross. And totally off subject, too.

"Oh, my! Yes! You must go over the bridge and across the lot, past the fountain, and turn left." The ill-dressed woman spoke in a thick, slow drawl. I could tell immediately that she was not quite right in the head but she was overjoyed to help us.

"Over the bridge, across the lot, pass the fountain, and turn left. Make sure you turn left," she repeated, her sing song lilt echoed off the buildings surrounding us. It made us an even greater spectacle than we already were.

"Okay, thank you very much!" Maynard grinned like a maniac as we walked away. As long as we were within earshot, we could hear her ho-hum voice still following us.

"Over the bridge, across the lot, past the fountain..." and waving her arms flagrantly to ensure we headed the right way.

We glanced over our shoulder, making sure she was out of sight before bursting into gales of laughter. She was so sweet, with her seemingly childish ways. We were about to have one humdinger of an argument, and she snapped us right out of it with her own special uniqueness. I couldn't stop thinking about her for days and the way she had lightened our whole outlook on life in that moment, which changed our countenance when we had nothing left to smile about. In that one moment she blessed us so much.

When we came back from our adventure, our friends had stopped in. We stared in question at the rather large suitcase they were dragging along behind.

"I mean, the hospital is great, but, are you planning to stay?" we laughed.

"Nope, not staying," they smiled, and unzipped the grand piece of luggage to expose a load of frozen TV dinners, snacks and beverages to last us a long time.

"Oh, wow! That is amazing, thank you so much!" we thanked them, humbled to be in this uncomfortable time of need in our life where it was necessary to accept help.

Our families were some of our greatest supporters. We felt understood by them when we didn't even understand ourselves. The kindly twinkle in my dad's eyes assured us that he loved us and supported us, when words may have fallen flat. Week after week my mom and Maynard's mom and sisters made sure we had an endless supply of delicious home cooked food or fresh baked cinnamon rolls. These gracious acts of generosity helped root us in the unfamiliar world we were forced to live in. They even came and stayed with Benny so we could spend time with the girls and explore Cleveland's many interesting sights. Our family never grew weary of coming to visit.

One day, Ellie brought pineapple rings. Pineapple rings are the crème de la crème. It is a dessert made by placing a slice of pineapple on a tray, then a nice, thick slice of soft caramel on top of that, *I'm talking a half inch thick if you're so lucky*, then pile it with whipped cream. Place a red cherry on top and voila!

"Ashley, want a pineapple ring?" we asked, eager to share this delicacy with our medical family.

"What is that?" she asked. "Is it some strange Amish food?"

"No! It's one of the most delicious desserts you will ever taste. Try it!" I exclaimed, dishing out a slice onto a plate for her and stabbing it with a fork.

"Okay," she hesitantly replied.

"Go ahead! You are going to eat *it*; <u>it</u> is not going to eat you!"

I watched her expression as she gingerly put a bite in her mouth and the combination of the pineapple and the caramel hit her taste buds.

"Oh, my goodness!" she exclaimed in delicious surprise, "This is to die for! Randy, come quickly!"

Randy came running.

"What is it?" he asked, looking about for the emergency.

Ashley stuck a fork full of pineapple ring into his face, and demanded that he taste it. He had no choice but to open his hatch as the food aimed for his mouth at full speed.

"Yum! It's amazing, but you're crazy! Don't do that again," he laughed, and dove for her plate in an attempt to steal it from her.

"Here, you can have this one," I said, and handed him a plate with the now famous pineapple ring.

He snatched it up, held it in the air and exclaimed as he went down the hall, "This is MY pineapple ring now!"

We had nurses and doctors come dashing for a taste, but they were too late. The pineapple rings were all gone. Well, except for the two with extra thick caramel which we had hid in the fridge for later!

And so it was that the medical team at Rainbow became our family away from home. We were really starting to love them. We laughed together, and we cried together. We even celebrated together.

"Maynard, what are we going to do? It's Hannah's birthday, and we don't have a gift," I said in disappointment not knowing how we were going to manage this special occasion.

Ashley overheard us and inquired, "What were you going to get her?"

"We were going to get her a personal CD player," we replied.

"Let me see what I can do. We have a roomful of donated items for situations just like this. I think I saw a CD player in there," she stated with a sparkle in her voice.

That evening when we were all in the room as a family, the whole nursing crew, and any other medical personnel they could rally, waltzed in singing Happy Birthday to Hannah. They had a birthday cake, balloons, and a beautifully wrapped gift.

Hannah's eyes popped open wide. She tore happily into her gift and exclaimed, "A CD player! A purple CD player! My very own! I can't believe it! Thank you!"

When Thanksgiving Day rolled around, the staff prepared a feast for anyone stuck in the 21 rooms in PICU.

Our family spent weeks inhabiting Benny's tiny room like it was a family den. It was a treat to be invited to the staff lounge where all manner of goodies were laid out. Even though we were away from home, it felt like a wonderful family celebration. The goodness of their hearts brought tears to our eyes. We knew it was an amazing hospital and staff to care enough to bless us so much.

At the other end of the spectrum were those well meaning folks who murmured how sorry they were, then offered the most stunning advice. This hospital was only using Benny for experiments, they said. It was clear to them we should just take him home to let him die.

He was on the ventilator, not even breathing by himself at the time, and so it was a little bit difficult for us to comprehend what they meant and how we were supposed to proceed. Honestly, I almost developed lock jaw from restraining my mouth from retaliation!

These well meaning folks also kindly informed us that we needed to stop fearing we would lose Benny. We were told that we needed to go home and be with our girls more. They alerted us to the "fact" that we were so afraid Benny would die, that we couldn't leave him. This would greatly affect our girls in the future, they said, and the girls would need extensive counseling to help them through this time of abandonment because we had directed all our time and energy towards Benny. In fact, they knew of children where this had happened.

We keenly felt that the criticism was directed towards our faith in God and were scorched right down to our souls. We searched our hearts and lives for an answer to our bewildering situation.

For the record, of course, we were fearful of losing our sweet baby who had fought so hard all his days of his little life. The main reason, though that one of us always stayed with him was because we never knew what would happen in that room if we weren't there to witness. This was very important to us. The nurses even spoke in favor of us always being there and of the value of having a parent there advocating for Benny all the time. The thought of leaving him there all by himself terrified us, so yes, we did have fear in that regard.

Many times, the doctors breathed down our throats in emergency situations, and we were forced to make split decisions. We nodded numbly sometimes, and other times we vehemently disagreed. We did the best we knew how, under tremendous stress.

And, so, the regular visits from our circle of friends dwindled to almost nothing. We weren't making the decisions they thought we should, and we began to feel detached from our community. We realized that we were on a journey, and had entered a world where our friends could not understand, or be able to join us. Our hearts felt like they were ripped out without anesthesia, and, sadly, we started to harbor a root of resentment towards them.

More than ever before, we turned to our biological families and to our medical family away from home.

It was during this time that we learned many life changing lessons. We learned not to judge someone who is walking through a baffling cloud of hurt, pain and confusion. Although they may not do things the way we think they should, they are walking this astounding road for the first time in their life.

We learned to never kick someone when they're down. All could be forgiven, but if they were only managing to survive, criticism from someone who had never been in their shoes had an enduring sting.

And last, but not least, we were at *Rainbow* Babies hospital. We would hold fast to the promise, and trust that our rainbow would one day become a shining light, faithful, strong and true, and all would be refreshed in a new world of hope. It was the promise to come after the storm.

EIGHT

Nurse Nancy

WE HAD ONE VERY SPECIAL nurse named Nancy. She was in charge! The first time she came into our room, I thought to myself, *She will either make or break this hospital stay.* Let's just say she made it! The first thing she did was make a list of the doctors and nurses and explained their order of authority. We had absolutely no hospital experience, so this was beyond helpful to us. Next she grabbed a stuffed bear and snuggled it beside Ben's face. It immediately softened the image of our Benny in his huge crib, and made the ventilator tubing seem less sterile and cold.

"Whoever did this IV was horribly sloppy," she said, gently undoing the IV bandages, and replacing them neatly. She made certain there were plenty of pampers, wipes, and formula right at our fingertips. The bedding was as neat as a pin and Benny always smelled nice.

"Oh, my, this blanket will never do. Benny needs a pretty one. I am going to the donation room and I will dig until I find just the right one," she tossed her words over her shoulder in her hurry to fetch the perfect blankie for Benny.

A few minutes later she dashed back into the room holding up her prize. "Check it out. Isn't this one so cute? Oh, I just love it, and Bobo will be adorable all wrapped up in it. Won't you, Bobo? Auntie Nancy will make you so comfy and cute! Look, Benny, it has a huge bear on it. Don't you love it? I knew you would, yes, I did!"

Benny squirmed and fretted against the ventilator tubing as if to say, *Sure enough I like the blanket with the life size brown teddy bear and all, but for heaven's sake, get these tubes out of my throat!*

"Whoops, he looked right at me, and he does not like these tubes. We are not even going there! KEYS! Who's got the keys? My Bobo needs a different sedative!" Nancy yelled as she marched toward the med cart with one mission on her mind; to obtain a different sedative for Benjamin.

"You can't have them," ordered the night nurse tiredly. "I already put a request in and they denied me!"

"Well. They won't deny me. They know better than to argue with Nancy! He needs a new sedative and I plan to get him one!"

And, oh, boy, she did. What a relief to see him fall asleep after many hours of torturous struggle. Nancy latched onto Benjamin, stood up for him, protected him, loved him, and kissed him with loud smacking kisses every day she was there.

"What are you doing in here?" challenged Nancy as Ashley strolled into our room and made a beeline towards Benny.

"Oh, nothing, except to kiss Benny," she smiled, bestowing smooches all over Benny's face.

"You can't come in here and kiss him! He is MY Bobo." demanded Nancy in jest.

"Stop it. He is not just your Bobo. He is mine, too, and I will come kiss him anytime I please. Anyway, he is the most kissed patient in this whole unit right now, so there," said Ashley, enforcing her words with her hands on her hips, daring Nancy to deny her the right to kiss Benny.

"Pf-ft, okay, then I guess you can come cuddle him." Nancy unwillingly obliged, with her nose in the air, glaring back in fun. She couldn't help but yell after Ashley as she strolled down the hall safely out of reach, "But he's still my Bobo!"

"You're impossible," we could hear Ashley protesting as she walked away.

Next the innocent, unsuspecting house doctor came in to do vitals, just as Benny had finally drifted off into a light sleep after much struggle.

"If you so much as touch him, I will crush all your bones to dust!" Nancy commanded in real fury this time.

The weary doctor glared at her defensively, and then he paused with his stethoscope in mid air, in a holding pattern above Benny's bare chest.

"I just want to listen to his lungs."

"Dust!" Nancy menaced, "You heard me! I will crush your bones to dust until there is only powder left! I mean it. Put that stethoscope away and get out! You don't need to listen to his lungs right this minute! I will let you know when you may come back in!"

Nancy was up to bat, with bases loaded, and she was aiming for a home run. She extended her arm out towards center field and knocked that ball totally out of the park, swinging that bat like Babe Ruth. Winner winner, chicken dinner! Ding de ding ding!

The doctor lumbered out of the room while scratching and shaking his shiny bald head and throwing an annoyed look across his shoulder. At least we think he looked. We were never quite sure with him. One eye was always going places it shouldn't, while the other eye seemed to stare off into cyber-space. I will never understand how he became a doctor. But he did, and he was actually one of our favorites.

One day, poor, clueless Rachel came in. She had already sat with the previous nurse and gotten the shift report and was now ready to settle in and be Benjamin's nurse for the day.

"What do you think you're doing? You don't get to be Benny's nurse. I'm sorry, but he is my Bobo and nobody else is his nurse while Nancy's here. Now scoot!" exclaimed Nancy, sailing in at the last minute, in disbelief that anyone should even dare do something so foolish.

"But I've already done reports from the night nurse! You weren't even on the schedule. Why are you even here?" argued Rachel in outrage at the brazen rudeness of Nancy.

"I am taking Molly's shift for her, and it makes absolutely no difference that you have done shift report, now go! I repeat: nobody gets Benjamin when I'm here!"

As Rachel left in a defeated huff, Nancy winked at us cheerfully. "I didn't make any friends that time around!"

We even got yelled at by her one miserable day. Benny had finally succumbed to sleep after much struggle against the ventilator tubing. Can we interrupt how we got yelled at and speak of great and terrible ventilators for a little bit? They are awful, horrible, yet needed beasts. Benny kept getting immune to the sedatives, making every minute torture, as he fought wildly in his weakened state, burning energy that he needed to get well. I could barely take it and when I hear prayer requests on Facebook from parents crying that God would allow the doctors to find a sedative that works for a precious child on a ventilator, I get on my knees to pray. Okay, on to the yelling...

Benny had finally fallen asleep, so we thought it would be a good time to go down to the cafeteria together. One of us always stayed with Benny. But this day we just wanted to eat together. While we were eating, our friends came to visit. Time passed so quickly and we stayed down much longer than we realized. When we made our way back to our room, a harried Nancy was there to greet us, blistering us with sores from the flames shooting from her eyes.

"There you are! Where have you been? Bobo has been crying all this time. He knows when you aren't here! Don't you ever do this to me again! He needs one of you here all the time!"

We swooped in on our darling boy, soothing and calming him immediately by rubbing his head and singing "Jesus loves Benny this I know." We purposed at that moment, sedated or not, he knows whether his family is by his side or not. We must always be there for this dear soul. What a precious child.

"Please can we try to wean Benjamin off the ventilator, so we don't have to fight it another whole weekend?" I heard the despair in Maynard's voice ringing loud and clear throughout the room. "I'm pretty sure he could be taken off."

It was Friday morning and we were quickly zoning into stress mode from battling the ventilator monster.

"I will try, Maynard, I will try. I am powerful but I am not God, and it will take an act from heaven for them to wean a patient on the weekend." Nancy stepped out of the room in search of the house doctor.

Hours later, she stepped back into the room, a surprised expression on her face. "I twisted, turned and prodded the arm of the head doctor, and she agreed to try weaning him if we do it right away this morning while full teams are still here. They will be coming in shortly and we will slowly start the process and see if he tolerates it. Happy dance, Troyers, happy dance!"

Wonder of wonders, by evening the ventilator was history and we were able to hold Benny. We were so glad we asked. We learned that we need not ever be afraid, intimidated, or too shy to ask at a hospital. They will say "no" if it's not possible, but sometimes all they need is involvement and interest from us as parents for that extra push. If we don't make known what we want or need, they will never know. We are our child's voice, his advocate, his protection to anything that happens in his room.

Oh, Nancy was an ornery one, but she was on our side wildly rooting for us and cheering us on. And so it was she that went downstairs with Benjamin to do a swallow study. There it was finally discovered that whenever he swallowed, his windpipe was collapsing because it was narrow and floppy, and because his jaw was retracted back too far. What a miracle that he had survived four months of this! I could hardly bear it when I thought of it. All those times he tried so hard to drink a bottle. He was hungry but it took so much effort to swallow and then gasp for air that it was the equivalent of us running a marathon. Can you imagine how difficult this was for him? This explained why he was drenched in sweat from his head of glossy black hair to impossibly tiny toe when he tried in vain to drink from a bottle. This also explained the difficulty he had breathing by himself and why he needed oxygen.

We sat in front of a medical team, going over everything they had found. He would be getting a feeding tube put in, have his hernias (ahem) repaired, and a trach placed, or surgery done to bring his jaw forward.

"Troyers, because Benny's jaw is so small and is back too far, this causes his already floppy and wiggly airway to collapse when he swallows. We can do surgery to bring his jaw out, but we don't recommend it in Benny's situation with him being so weak to begin with. We would have to wait weeks until he is strong enough, and even then it is a terrible surgery to recover from for someone who is hearty and strong. Are you following what we're saying so far?"

We nodded in affirmation.

"The next option, which we favor, is placing a trach. The trach is a small piece of tubing placed in the trachea. He will then breathe through this completely. This will give his jaw a chance to grow out by itself over time. Our experience is around five to six years."

As the doctors explained this to us they carefully watched our reaction.

"By all means, put a trach in! We are not afraid of a trach. We have a nephew with a trach and have watched his parents care for him and we are sure we are able to do this. Yes, by all means put it in!" we confidently exclaimed.

The doctors looked at us incredulously, as if they had just won a million dollar lottery ticket.

"You are the first people to *ever* say that! Most people want to banish us off the face of the earth when we tell them their child needs a trach." They could hardly believe their good fortune.

"But do you fully understand the intense care this will take? This airway must be kept clear at all times, or he will suffocate. Someone needs to be with him every single moment, literally, to suction his airway when it gets full. It needs to be kept immaculately clean, or infection will set in. The first 3 months you will need to pull the trach and put a new one in every week."

Eep! My eyes grew as big as ping pong balls. Pull the trach and put a new one in? Um ...I glanced at Maynard. He was.... wait....smiling?

"That's not a problem at all," I heard him say through the fog of thick smog that had invaded my brain and was telling me to collapse into an unceremonious pile at their feet. I imagined pulling myself up by my boot strings and realized I hadn't actually collapsed, but instead, was standing on my own two feet nodding my head in agreement. I wondered if I would ever live a normal life again. Ever. Everything was so overwhelming! I felt hot all over. Would I actually be able to do this? Pull the trach and put a new one in? How hard could it be? Right in that moment it looked so hard that impossible was a word that wanted to invade my muddled mind and stake a claim.

When we got back to our room we called Maynard's sister, Ruby, right away.

"Guess what? Benjamin is getting a trach just like Arlin!" we burst the news to her unsuspecting ears as if we had just won a prize.

"What? I can't believe it! Well, I'm telling you right now, you can do it. Trach care isn't nearly as hard as people think," she said, encouraging us.

The staff immediately scheduled Benjamin for surgery. The plan was that he would be going in on Friday morning, and would need to be prepped for surgery all night long in order to be ready to go.

The medical team had also finally presented us with a diagnosis for Benjamin. They said he had Beals Syndrome. The medical terminology for Beals Syndrome is this: "Congenital, (born with it), Contractural, (contracted joints) Arachnodactyly, (abnormally long fingers and toes). It described Benjamin to a "T".

"Because of Benjamin's contracted joints, he may never walk. If he does he will walk like this." Dr. Nelson had explained and demonstrated by hunching over at her waist and bending her knees and kind of bouncing along.

It made me feel ill at ease to see this demonstration of how Benny might walk one day. It felt like an unfamiliar world that was terrifying and strange had been assigned to us. What would the future hold for our sweet baby?

We enjoyed our time holding Benny, wrapping him up in his

blankie with the big-as-life bear. The girls always came for their regular weekend stay. The doctors observed that Benny always perked up when they came around.

We took turns staying with Benny while the other would go take the girls to the local museums and even the zoo. At night, one of us always stayed at the hospital with Benny, while the other took the bus to the Ronald McDonald house. We loved going there. There were no beeping machines. There was a soft warm bed, and a private shower. There was always good food to eat, and usually people to visit, with such interesting stories to share.

On one such occasion, a lady listened to our story about Benny, and how he would likely need heart surgery in the future.

"I want you to take this CD home with you. They are all verses of healing through song from Psalms. Play it quietly in the background of your home whenever you can. These healing words from scripture will heal Benny's heart." She sounded so confident.

"Oh, thank you!" I exclaimed, tucking the CD in my satchel. I never saw her again. It was like she had an appointment to meet me there and then go on with her life. I marveled at such an odd happening, and pondered it in my heart, praying she was right and that Benny's heart would be healed.

NINE
Surgeries and Rubber Dolls

ONE DAY WE GOT new neighbors in the room next to us. God himself put them there. Their daughter was 21 years old. It was an unheard of age to be in PICU.

After observing for a few days I connected with Nurse Nancy.

"Why is she here in PICU if she's 21 years old?" I questioned. The "P" in PICU stood for pediatric, and her age disqualified her from that, but I knew there must be a reason.

"Oh, dear," replied Nancy. "She has a terminal lung-disease. They brought her down from the adult ICU so the family could have a private room for her passing."

I felt devastated and grieved for this dear family and watched for an opportunity to reach out to them.

I was there by myself most of the weekdays, so I did get the chance to meet them. I tried to encourage them, not with any fancy words, but simply by hugging them when we passed in the halls, letting them know I cared deeply for their terrible pain that no parent ever should have to face. I brought them coffee when I went to get some or cold bottled waters.

"Would you like to meet our son?" I invited.

"We would love to," they heartily agreed.

I brought them in to see Benny. He was sound asleep, and covered with his bear blanket, in the nest Nancy had made for him.

They stood by his bedside and wept.

"You want to know what we see when we look at him?" they inquired brokenly.

I nodded with tears in my eyes.

"We see hope. Despite all the machines, needles and tape, we see hope. He has a chance. He can live! Thank you so much for allowing us to see him. We are refreshed to still see the promise of life. Though it is too late for our daughter, it is not too late for Benjamin. God bless you as you take care of him!"

A few hours later, all doors and curtains in the whole unit were pulled shut. An air of respectful reverence permeated the block of rooms as the coroner wheeled out the now pain-free body of our dear neighbor. I took a deep breath, visualizing the amazing lung capacity she had just earned by stepping through heaven's glitzy gates. Sadly, I never saw any of them again. But they still live in my heart.

Surgery day to repair Benjamin's hernias, place his feeding tube, and his trach drew nearer. We were eager to move into the next phase and begin our training so we could go home. It was obvious by Benjamin's breathing that he needed that trach. The nurses commented that he always wore a worried expression on his brow and attributed this to his troubled respiratory system.

Finally the big day dawned for the scheduled surgery. We saw teams of doctors on Benjamin's case prepping him for hours, and we were feeling anxious and a little bit frightened.

"We have to cancel the surgery." It was Ashley that came running to breathlessly give us the bad news.

"What are you talking about? We just put Benny through hours of prepping!" We were dismayed and disheartened.

"Something came up and we have to reschedule. The surgeon performing the hernia repair was incorrectly informed, and he can't perform the surgery this morning. I'm so sorry," sighed Ashley. "It is a bit challenging because of the three combined surgeries all in one shot. Otherwise we would be able to do it, but we need a fully equipped team for something so complex."

It was already Friday morning, so this meant the surgery wouldn't be until next week. We had another weekend to endure. It looked like a mountain.

"But this is a big hospital, and mistakes like this should not happen!" The wee little lady, (me), with too much spunk for her own good erupted in frustration.

"Sit down with me, Mom and Dad, because I want to share something with you," said Ashley calmly. "I have worked here a long time, and I have seen many things. I can assure you that this is the hand of God. This hardly ever happens, and when it does, there is a reason to the benefit of the patient. I know it seems hard and unfair, and we will never know for sure how it got communicated wrongly. But know this, the right surgeon that God wanted for Benny wasn't here, or maybe the right doctor was here, but he was too exhausted in God's eyes to do the perfect job for Benny. God has only the best in mind for our Bobo, and this morning didn't meet up to God's standard for some reason."

We nodded in weary agreement as we took in this sermon-ette. Although we were still disappointed, we had peace that this was meant to be.

"And so tonight," continued Ashley, "I am taking care of Benjamin, and you are both taking the evening off, and you will spend the night together at Ronald McDonald house. I will sit beside him all night. I promise. I don't have any other patient tonight, and I got this. You go. I insist." Ashley was determined.

One of the other nurses sauntered up declaring her loyalty to pitch in and help where needed and we should go take an evening off.

We felt like naughty young kids, but we acquiesced and sailed away to the Ronald McDonald house, ate a hearty supper, brought in by a local church youth group, and just enjoyed being together in peace and quiet.

A Ronald McDonald House is that "home away from home" for families so they can be together and stay close by their hospitalized child at little or no cost. Being able to have this time with our girls on weekends was a healing time for us. Along with hot, home cooked meals, they had a weekly craft class that our girls enjoyed. It is all made possible by generous volunteers and donors.

We went up to our room sprawling across the burgundy floral bedspread basking in the most amazing thing called privacy. While we were there, we got to talking about how much we had learned through this whole ordeal.

"What has stood out to you the most through all this?" probed Maynard gently.

"For me, it is the fact that we have lived a much protected life," I began. "We have managed to put God in a box when He is so much bigger than that. We have been ministered to by the most unlikely people. People that we may have thought are living a worldly life because of the way they dress or the church they attend, have ministered to our hearts, and lifted our spirits. I feel like we have lived a self righteous life, and I am so done with it. I want to be able to see God outside of the little box I have created, and allow his light to shine wherever we may be, and whatever we may be going through."

"Yes! Me, too," exclaimed Maynard enthusiastically. "We

have been so small minded and we need to step out and embrace God in all things. Especially the unlikely people you mentioned. Like when Ashley encouraged us so generously. They have been like balms to our souls. Every day when Willie comes in to clean Ben's room, he prays with us, and blesses Benny. And our neighbors with the tattooed arms touched our hearts with their daughter passing, and the hope they saw in Benny. And the lady that gave you the CD for Benny's healing. How amazing that we had God in such a small box, that when we walked into this hospital we looked at each other and said *this is a God forsaken place!* We have found God here in a new way, through his people he has specifically placed in our paths."

And so began a renewed vision, and we have been on a journey with God ever since. This has made us stand out at times, but God faithfully teaches us and reminds us time after time not to be self righteous, and to accept people as they are. He tells us in his quiet voice when we are stepping dangerously close to the ugly self righteous pile he calls filthy rags. Who wants to be close to filthy rags? Smelly, dirty, stained and ugly. If God calls them filthy, he must really not like them at all. Zero. Zilch. Nada.

Every Friday when I clean my house, I put all the dirty rags on a pile as I get done with them. They are not pretty, and can smell pretty wretched. I always let it remind me to stay away from the filthy rags God calls my own self righteousness.

Did I just say I clean my house every Friday? Make that I intend to clean my home every Friday. I hear laughing. Someone somewhere is totally snorting. On with the story...

The next morning we got up bright and early, feeling refreshed and ready to face another day in Hospital World. Everyone was happy, and Benny had a good night without any breathing episodes. Surgery was scheduled for the next Tuesday, and we were able to begin our training today!

Our first training session was with trached rubber dolls. They were floppy and oddly heavy. These dolls had supposedly quit breathing. We were to walk up to the crib, discover they weren't breathing, whack them sharply on the chest, and scream, "Oh baby!" and start resuscitation via the trach. So because I don't ever do anything half ways, and because I am hailed a drama queen, when it was my turn, I did just as I was told. I sauntered casually up to the crib where my flabby rubber doll was supposed to be taking a leisurely siesta. But, lo! She was not breathing. I up and whacked that slack rubber baby on the chest for all I was worth, all while yelling at the top of my voice, "Oh baby!" And just like that, without even resuscitating it, that rubber doll decided to spring back to life! Welcome back, baby! No, for real, I did attach the bagger to the doll's trach and began resuscitating it. One, two, three breaths with the bagger, then she started moving air. I guess that's what brought it back to life, but I'm convinced the whack helped, too!

I thought our instructor would collapse from laughing so hard. "Well that was great, girl! You need to go to Hollywood and become an actor. You're good!" she guffawed.

I'm guessing all the pent up emotions from the past few months landed squarely on that dear rubber doll. Also, Maynard was probably acting like he didn't know me from Adam had I peered over my shoulder. For all I know, he was holding a sign that said *this is not the wife of my youth.*

For some reason, that instructor never forgot me. Whenever we met in the hallways or the Atrium, she would give a big smile and wave, "Hi, Mrs. Troyer!"

"She remembers my name," I told Maynard.

"How could she ever forget?" laughed Maynard. "She probably has rubber doll whacking nightmares!"

The training continued, and the next scheduled surgery day

came and Benny was whisked off to the operating room. As my child disappeared into the sterile chill behind the steel doors, the air was sucked out of my lungs. I reached for Maynard's hand as we walked slowly back to Benjamin's room to wait his return.

The phone rang. We were glad for a distraction, anticipating someone would call with words of encouragement while Benny was in surgery. Instead, it was one of those well meaning calls instructing us on the grave mistakes we were making and how to order our hospital life with Benny. We sat in silence for a minute after hanging up, until we could successfully squash down the urge to open our mouths and voraciously scream in our own defense. Our confidence lagged as we adjusted to the barrage of well-intended criticism thrown our way that caused us to wake up in cold sweats for months afterward.

It was tempting to think that even God had chosen to turn his back on us.

"We can forgive because they don't know what they're saying, honey," murmured Maynard into the still shocked silence. "It is the only way. Otherwise we will just become bitter. I will call them back later and try to reason with them."

"Yes, I know, but it's hard." I spoke quietly.

Maynard nodded his head and reached out to give me a quick hug.

I was thankful that Nancy was there when Benjamin came back to his room. She had a small heat blower ready, and stuck it under his blankets to warm him up from being in the cold operating room. She made sure he was cozy and comfortable. The bed was as neat as a pin. The doctor's orders were to keep him sedated and on the ventilator for at least two days to keep him from tearing out the trach. He had three wound sites, so he struggled with fevers in the fight to heal the incisions. He needed medication to fight the fevers, which then gave him nasty rashes and diarrhea. More medication was given to combat those issues which led to other issues that needed medication. I'm telling you, it's a vicious cycle, leading one around in circles for days.

One thing I hadn't realized is that once he had the trach, the ventilator would be attached to that. No yucky tubes down his throat! I was beyond thankful for this tiny little blessing.

A few times as the sedation started to wear off, he would cry a little bit. It seemed normal except there was absolutely no vocal sound. We are so miraculously created, that unless our exhaling air goes over our vocal chords, we have no voice at all. It so happens that a trach is placed right under the vocal chords, so Benny could yell and scream and carry on and we would still not hear a sound.

It broke my heart to think of not hearing his voice for as long as he had the trach. The doctors told us it would probably be five years or more. I needed to take one day, and one moment at a time. Five years was too long. So I put it away and let it go. Today I would care for my Benny. He couldn't make any vocal sounds, but I absolutely could love him.

After a few days, he was once again weaned off the vent, and the sedation wore off. Everyone was excited to see how Benny would respond.

"Okay, Mom, let's see how he does with a bottle now that he can breathe. Have you noticed that he isn't wearing the worry on his face anymore?" Nancy was almost dancing. "He looks so much more relaxed, and it's all because he has that trach, and he is free to breathe. You hold him and we will see if he still sweats up a storm while drinking a bottle."

Benjamin eagerly took the bottle and began hungrily sucking for all he was worth. He never stopped once to catch his breath. He didn't need to. Since he was doing all his breathing through his trach, he could just drink nonstop. That whole two ounces went down his little hatch without a droplet of sweat anywhere. His dark smoky eyes looked at me triumphantly like he had just climbed Mt. Everest without skipping a beat. *Look at me go, Mom! I got this now!* I beamed back at him and told him what an amazing little Benny Boy he was for being so brave and strong.

My aunt and uncle had come to visit, all the way from Florida, and they were there to witness and celebrate with us this moment. They smiled and rejoiced with us in our new-found success. We were so thankful for family to walk beside us, celebrating as we claimed one victory at a time.

Recovery from sedation was pretty traumatic for Benjamin. He just quit sleeping. For four solid days and nights he didn't as much as nod off. How we longed for him to fall asleep! Instead he fussed and whined and carried on without a sound except for hissing noises from his trach. We learned trach sounds in a blitz. We watched the nurses and became brave enough to just pick up the catheter and quickly relieve him of a clogged airway when they weren't readily available. It wasn't very difficult at all. We soon realized we were just as good, if not better, at it than they were.

"Mrs. Troyer, you have a phone call." The intercom buzzed into my sleep deprived brain.

"Hello?"

"Hey, Marietta, this is Mom. I am just calling to let you know that Dad, Ruby and I are coming tomorrow and we will stay in Benjamin's room all day. You take the girls and go out and do some fun stuff!"

"That sounds amazing!" I exclaimed, "We accept, but I'm warning you, Benny is fussy and he doesn't sleep at all."

"Don't worry about it. We sleep all night in our beds at home and we are good to go. I'm sure you are tired though." Mom said with compassion.

"Yes, for sure. We are pretty hazy brained!" I answered. *Hazy brained. Who even says that?* I thought to myself. *Oh yeah, hazy brained, exhausted people do.*

I found myself worrying about suctioning. Would the nurses be there in time? Maybe we shouldn't leave.

"Honey, this is a hospital. He will be fine without us. They suctioned him all the time before we learned how," said Maynard confidently, but I could detect a note of apprehension in him as well.

How had we learned so quickly what had seemed so scary and impossible? We had assumed responsibility and it was frightening to let it go, but we decided it was pretty mother hen-ish and selfish of us to think the PICU staff couldn't do it, so we planned to take off and let my parents and my sister take over.

The day dawned bright and sunny and very cold as the wind from Lake Erie swooped in and wrapped itself around us in its unforgiving dampness. We strolled through the town and enjoyed seeing the Christmas decorations and storefronts. We spent all day together as a family, and when we came back to the hospital, we expected to see weary parents and sister.

"Benjamin fell asleep and hasn't moved since you left!" announced Dad as we stepped back into the room.

We stood in open mouthed amazement at this declaration.

"Let's hope he stays asleep now!" smiled Maynard.

I don't think he meant he should sleep for two days, but that's what happened. We had to wake him up for any therapy. He was fed mostly by continuous tube feeds. We could barely get him awake enough for bottle feeds.

Benjamin continued to improve and our training was almost done. Maynard and I both had to change the trach three times before we would be allowed to go home, and we had yet to climb this last looming mountain. One day Dr. Teebow came in to Benjamin's bedside. He set up a new trach, pulled the old one out and said, "Okay, Mom, put the new one in."

"Wha...bu..uh..."

I noticed Benny squirming and sputtering sounds were coming from the stoma. *Thanks for the warning, old boy!* With the speed of a race horse, I grabbed the new sterile trach the doctor had set up, and I put it back in Benjamin's neck just like I had practiced on the floppy rubber dolls. My legs felt more wobbly than a new born colt but I managed to stay in a vertical position. Since I have a tradition of fainting only after giving birth, I didn't pass out after it was all said and done. But I wanted to. I wanted to fall flat on my face to give that otolaryngologist a lesson he wouldn't soon forget.

The next day when Nancy heard about the stunt the doctor had pulled; she whirled around and planned on hunting that poor soul down.

"No, Nancy, it was fine. I'm okay. It was scary to have it thrust on me without warning like that, but I survived, and now I have only two trach changes to go before we can go home. Leave him be."

"But that is unheard of! He can't get away with that. They never ever do that to anyone," she insisted.

I shook my head, "No, let it go."

Nancy relented, albeit unwillingly. But she still had another opportunity later that day to jump to my defense.

Earlier that day, Sophia, a social worker, had come in.

"You must sign on to have a 24 hour nurse at your house," she demanded.

"But I don't want a caregiver at my house all day and all night." I fired back.

"You have to. There is no way anyone can care for him like he needs to be cared for. You will never sleep. I promise. Please, Mrs. Troyer, sign here for a nurse." She was beginning to sound angry.

"I know we can care for Benny by ourselves at home. Let us try. If we see it's not possible, we will be humble enough to call someone, but we want to at least try." I relentlessly stood my ground.

She turned around and left the room without a word.

Nancy caught me in tears, nursing my wounds as I repeated to her all that Sophia had insisted.

"That's unreasonable," stated Nancy emphatically. "You basically do all the trach care already here in the room. Of course you can do it!"

She turned around and left the room only to come back with Sophia humbly in tow. How do I know it was humbly? Because Sophia had her crew neck sweater pulled up all the way to the top of her short cropped hair.

"Apologize. Now," ordered Nancy, giving her a gentle shove into the room.

Sophia pulled the brown sweater down just so her hazel eyes peeked out. "Mrs. Troyer, I am so sorry for upsetting you. You may try going home without a nurse. Apology accepted?" she smiled apprehensively and slid a quick glance at Nancy.

I couldn't help but burst into laughter, "Apology accepted, and thank you!"

"You're welcome!" She turned around to face Nancy. "May I leave now, Nancy?"

"You may leave, but don't you ever offend my kids again, you hear?" responded Nancy with a glower.

Sophia turned around to leave. I mouthed a *thank you* to Nancy as she hurried off to answer an intercom call.

As we mastered the skills on the checklist, we were almost to the point of discharge. One last meeting with every specialist, and a rundown on all the machines and the lights of home were beckoning; a faint promising glimmer in the distance.

BENNY
Pictures Through the Years

Maynard and I in 1990.
A few months before we got married.

Our first child, Diana,
at 3 months old.

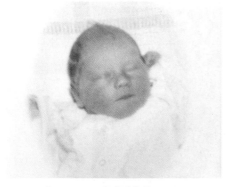

Our second child, Laurie,
at 1 day old.

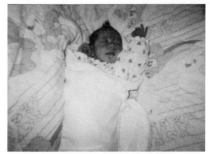

Our third child, Hannah,
at 2 weeks old.

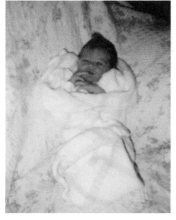

Our fourth child, Samantha,
at 2 days old.

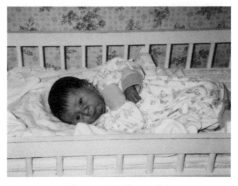

Benny! 8 days old.

We just finished singing, "I'm a Little Miracle."

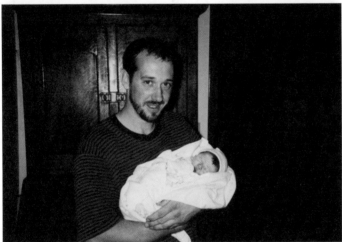

Maynard holding his first son.

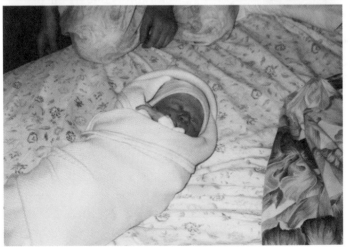

Bennal all wrapped up and ready to go!

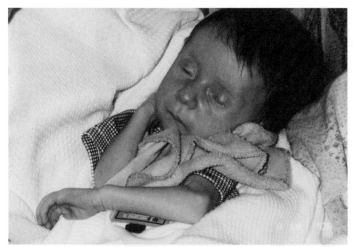

My dear baby kept getting skinnier...

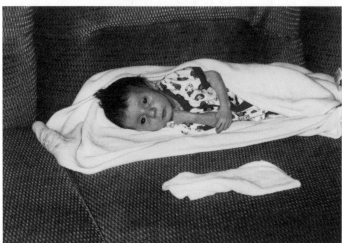

... and skinnier. These pictures are a few days before we finally got help.

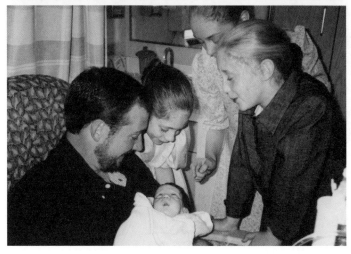

At the hospital the first time before being transferred to Rainbow.

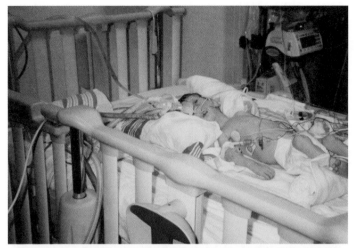

At Rainbow before Nurse Nancy came on the scene.

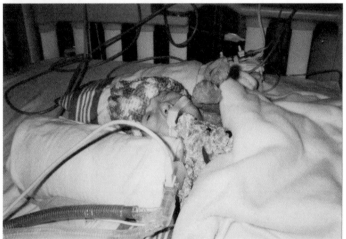

After Nurse Nancy; all snuggled up with a bear on one side and a bunny on the other.

The ventilator is off and he's finally in our arms.

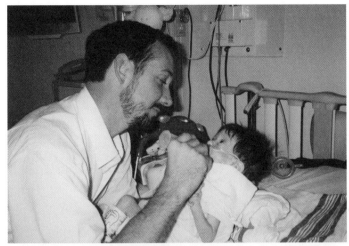

At Rainbow before the trach, trying a bottle feed.

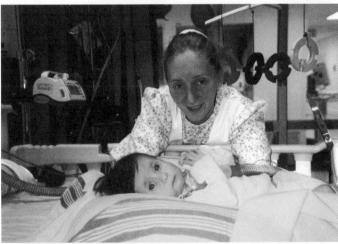

After the trach. He is looking so much more relaxed.

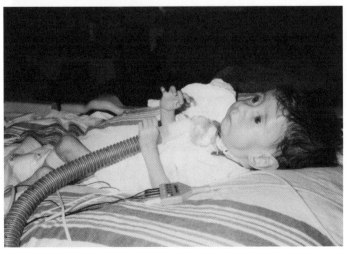

Getting used to this thing called a trach.

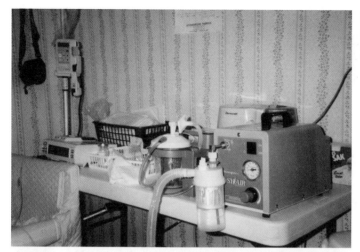

Our bedroom turned into a hospital.

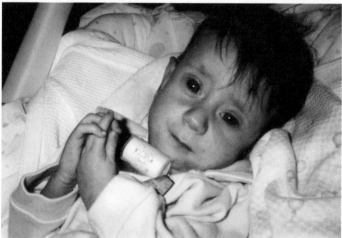

Benny at home.

A moment with mom.

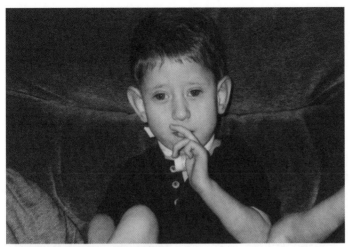

Benny,
2 years old.

Benny, 3 years old.

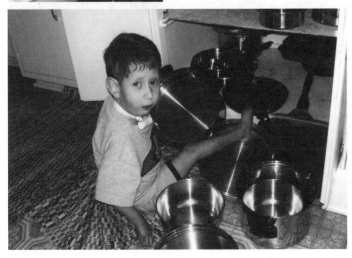

Benny,
4 years old.

Benny,
6 years old
with his
favorite
person on
earth; Daddy!

Our miracle Benny today!

TEN

Coming Home and Recognizing Our Call

AS I WATCHED the glitzy hospital disappear in the rear view mirror it felt like a walk on the white sands of a balmy Florida beach. After 42 days, the three combined surgeries, and weeks of daunting training regarding his medical needs, we bade a tearful goodbye to the amazing staff at Rainbow and headed for home, sweet home!

Before we made it out the door, though, Nurse Nancy pulled me aside.

"Mrs. Troyer, I want you to hear it from me, so you will be prepared for what is in your future. Unfortunately, you will be back often."

She held up her hand upon seeing the dismay in my troubled baby blues beneath my furrowed brows.

"Look, I know you're excited to go home, and it seems like it will be happily ever after, but Benjamin has a ton of issues. He has two wound sites on his body, from the trach and the feeding tube. These are little infection bombs just waiting to happen. I wish you the very best, but see you back soon! Love you all to the moon and back." She turned to Benny, "Goodbye, my Bobo baby boy, honey pooh, sweetie pie. I love you so much. Come back to see Nancy, okay?" she smacked him with kisses too many to count and hurried away, but not before I saw the tears running down her cheeks.

Benjamin sported a trach, a feeding tube and newly repaired hernias. Apprehension was creeping in as we unloaded our collection of machines, monitors, oxygen, IV poles and medical supplies. Our bedroom turned into a hospital room as we rearranged and organized to make room for all the monitors and huffing, puffing machines, all attached somehow to our tiny baby boy. The supplies that plugged silently into the walls behind the hospital bed in his PICU room were now visible, noisy machines right by our bedside. I had the misgiving feeling that sleep as we knew it was over and done. Still unfamiliar with the machines, the alarms seemed to go off nonstop all the nights long. We were both up all night trying to figure out the new, shocking, exhausting way of living thrust our way. On top of all that, Benjamin didn't transition well from hospital to home, constantly crying for reasons we couldn't figure out, except that the machines needed adjusted. Again.

After it all calmed down, we took turns sleeping every other night. We soon learned that indeed, we were tired enough, that when it was our turn to sleep, we didn't even hear the background noise constantly whirring and beeping their way through the night, as the better half took over.

Exhausted from this new regimen, I remembered Sophia and her insistence on a twenty-four hour nurse, and I was tempted to call her. Then I thought of that nurse being in our home around the clock, and I knew that would only add more stress.

Upon coming home, we decided that Diana and Laurie would be trained for suctioning and tube feeding right away.

106

They were eager to learn to help out with Benny. They did a tremendous job for as young as they were. They were only ten and eleven years old, but learn it they did! Even Hannah (five) and Samantha (three), quickly learned the gurgling, wheezing sounds coming from Benjamin's trach, and knew the moment he needed suctioned.

Many times I would be in the kitchen cooking supper and would hear their young voices yell at the top of their lungs, "Mom, suction!" and I would come dashing from the kitchen to perform the duty!

It took us approximately three months to completely settle in and be comfortable with the new normal. Sometimes I try to block out this part of our Benny memories. It was so frustrating, and difficult.

One extremely trying day, when the alarms went off constantly, causing many anxious moments, one of my friends called to see how it was going.

"Hey, there, how are things going for you over there? I bet you're so happy to be home!" she basically sang into the phone, expecting a glorious, spiritual response in return.

"Yes, we are glad to be home, but actually it's really hard," I said, the tears in my throat blocked my vocal cords so they came out first in high pitched squeaks, then dropped to bass level lows all on the same syllable, as if I was trying out for choir practice. She must have decided right then and there that I couldn't be anywhere near her perfect choir, and that she needed an unwavering, clear tone, because she had business to attend to suddenly and had to go.

Although she didn't say it in actual words, this is what I heard. *I am sick and tired of your problems. All you do is complain and cry. Get over it, girl. Your life isn't that hard. Move on. I don't have time for this.* Then she went about her perfectly normal day, in her flawless corner of the world.

This conversation turned me just a tad bit hard and cold. In my overwhelmed heart, I pledged to never share again. In that moment I let a seed of bitterness start to grow inside, which began to turn my heart into a chilly bit of steel. I have seen it in many situations since. People get tired of reaching out to others after a long period of time. The need doesn't become less, but the desire to help does. Then when the people in need become indifferent, and reach out to other folks that they don't necessarily approve of, they are nailed about their lack of spiritual discernment. Bam! And the vicious cycle is on a roll, crushing hearts as it goes.

Our marriage suffered in ways we never thought possible. It was a tricky thing to walk daily without ruffling the other's feathers. In fact, sometimes we wanted to tar and feather each other! How's that for an honest look into our not so harmonious stage of Benny-life?

"Honey, you didn't attach his feed correctly. Benny is laying in a half inch of formula right now. His whole room smells like rotten milk-replacer. Now I have to bathe him all over again and change his trach tie and the entire bedding, too. It's all sopping wet. Help me unravel him from the machines, quick, and strip him down," I fumed. "Honey, did you hear?"

"Yes, I heard. I'm coming, calm down butter cup, it's not the end of the world," Maynard retorted wearily, "and I did attach it correctly, he must have squirmed his way out of it."

"Don't call me butter cup," I glowered menacingly.

Maynard shrugged, "Whatever, baby doll."

Then we fell into a fit of giggles. This is kind of how we rolled. You could tell where we had been by tracking the trail of angry words and accusations, followed immediately by giggles, as we realized how foolish we sounded. The giggle moments are what saved our respect and love for each other. The very last thing we could afford to do was let our hearts grow cold towards each other.

The disruption of every day routines with the constant need for change caused not only our marriage to suffer but also our family life.

The only way to get any homeschooling done was to get up at 4:30am and have it done by the time Maynard left for work at 7:00. He had sold his milk route, and was working on a local construction crew so he wasn't as tied down as before. So we got up at the insane and unappealing hour of 4:30, and we did school and were done with most of it by seven. The easy stuff could be stuck in throughout the day.

"Mom, I can't seem to get this math problem figured out," said Diana as she strolled up to the rocking chair I was using to hold Benny as I tried a bottle feed.

"Sure, let me help," I reached out for her book.

"Mom!" yelled Diana frantically.

"What?" I looked around trying to find the reason for such panic.

She pointed with shaky fingers at Benny's hand. I looked down and there he was, calmly holding his entire G-tube, blood dripping from the end where it had been attached to his skin only moments before.

"Oh, no! He pulled out his feeding tube! What do I do?" I moaned, frightened out of my wits as my mind scrambled to all rubber doll training and what my options were.

"I don't know, Mom! Do something! Will he die?" Diana's sobs alerted the troops and they all descended toward the rocking chair, and simultaneously burst into tears at Diana's morbid question.

"No he won't die. It will be okay. I remember them teaching

us that if we don't replace a pulled tube in two hours we will need to perform surgery again. I don't have another tube, and I don't have a vehicle. I will call 911, and they can take us to the emergency room and put one in for us at the hospital." I determined this to be the best course of action.

I dialed 911, and then arranged for the girls to stay with dear, faithful Ellie once again.

At the hospital, they decided a Mic-key button was a better arrangement for us instead of the tube. The compact package of a button was so much more convenient, and we looked at this episode as a blessing in disguise.

"It sure messed up our day, but this works so much better that that ugly brown tube always coming loose and flooding the bed, causing you to yell at me," teased Maynard.

"You bet!" I bantered back with a smile, as I reached for the catheter to suction the gurgling trach.

To top it all off, our relationship with our church had become strained. Personally, I was not able to attend a church service for four months. I had no desire to go or to fellowship with other believers. I felt very misunderstood. Granted, there were also times where we made mistakes, and we misunderstood the way our church family responded, as well. There was misunderstanding on both sides and it began to drive a wedge. We had entered an unfamiliar world and to walk with us meant tip-toeing a fine line. We acknowledge this, and look ahead and not behind!

That being said, one church family stopped in to see us after church. When they learned that one of us sat beside Benny all the time, 24 hours a day, they moved into action.

"This will never do. You can't sit here all the time!" they exclaimed.

"We take turns on two hour shifts, so it's not so bad," we replied.

Nevertheless, one week later, they had equipped us with a camera in Ben's room and a screen monitor to carry with us to other parts of the house. The freedom was so amazing! We could fold laundry or bake cookies and keep an eye on him at the same time! We used it for years and years before it gave out, and by then we could do without it. Before we had this gadget, I cut fabric for my many sewing projects right on top of the bed, suctioning as I went, or pushing meds through his tube. I even cut the bedspread accidentally, leaving a gaping hole as a prized souvenir!

Two years before, this very same family had prophesied into our lives. One Sunday after church, Gary had pulled Maynard and me to the side of the fellowship hall.

"I have a word from the Lord for you. I don't know what it means, but I must tell you. You will have a special ministry. What it is, I don't know. Just prepare your hearts and pray the Lord will reveal it to you one day."

We were so excited, and prayed many times for wisdom and discernment that when our ministry came our way, we would not miss it! What if it was an amazing trip across the ocean? Or a prison ministry to reach thousands? Africa? Mexico? Asia? Would we become great missionaries with impressive stories to tell? We couldn't wait for God to reveal it so we could begin our journey.

One evening after an especially trying day, Maynard reflected, "Remember how Gary prophesied into our lives about a special ministry coming our way a few years ago?"

"Yes, I remember," I hesitantly replied.

"This is it! It's Benjamin, I just know it."

"Could it be? But it's so unnoticed and small, and yet at the same time, it's incredibly huge. What an easy ministry to love and care for our Benny!"

"Why, yes!" Maynard exclaimed as the light dawned brighter

in his eyes at this revelation.

It would be easy and extremely difficult at the same time. We would not be going overseas or to a prison ministry anytime soon. We would instead be "stuck" at home, seemingly small and unnoticed, caring for a child that needed us desperately. A child we as a family loved more than we ever thought possible. It has never occurred to us to feel disappointed. It is our call in life, and we are totally fulfilled to minister and care for our Benny in any way possible.

My family often came to visit. My brother watched as we took care of Benjamin all day. One evening, before he left he approached me quietly.

"One day, I will tell Benjamin how well you took care of him when he needed you so much," he said as emotions clouded his voice.

"Thank you, Joe, that is so nice of you to say so," I answered tearfully.

"I mean every word. You are doing an amazing job. Not every child is as blessed as Benjamin."

Small and unnoticed? I don't think so. Right then I felt like I had the most important ministry and calling that an American girl could obtain. Let missionaries go overseas by the Mayflower ship loads, and the singers and preachers go into the prisons in their big, floating buses. Let great and noble Billy Grahams win souls by the hundreds in massive stadiums with booming sound systems. God bless them as they fulfill their call. I have been called to stay put and minister to my Benny.

The revelation lit a fire in our souls, and we were at peace with our life mission.

One day I shared with my best friend, Ellie, about a difficult day with Benny. Then I felt bad for complaining and apologized. She took hold of my shoulders and said, "Let me tell you something, dear friend. We can all see this is hard. If you would come glowing all the time, never shedding any tears, and have all good reports on how wonderful it is to have a special needs child, I would send you to a counselor because something would be wrong with that. But because you are honest, and share both the good and the bad, I know you are okay."

I can't even begin to describe the deep thankfulness I garnered from her words. Years later I still go back to this day to listen in once again on this conversation.

When I shared with my mom about this life changing talk, she said, "That is a good friend. You better hang on to her."

Amen!

One day, Benjamin started vomiting out of the blue. I became so attuned to this that I could "hear" his silent projections from two rooms away and with the doors firmly shut.

This was not the baby spit the parenting books talk about. It wasn't even the projectile vomit mentioned as the worst kind of infant throw-up in the books. It was epic hurling that deserves to be composed in song, and hitting the number one spot of a music chart somewhere for years.

"Mom! Puke!" yelled Diana frantically.

"I'm coming!" I shouted back from the garden. I dropped my hoe and ran barefoot across the brown, freshly tilled dirt and leaped over bean plants and one foot high corn.

"Hold his head, Diana, while I try to keep it all contained in one place. Laurie, grab the suction machine, quickly! Oh, no, there we go. It got all over his trach ties. Into the bath you go, Benny. Here, Hannah, please throw all the blankets and his clothes in the washer for me."

In all my six pregnancies combined, and with all my vicious tummy dumping going on at that time, I never threw up as much as Benjamin did in this two year period of his life. It was probably eight ounces at a time, many times a day. Each time we had to strip and wash everything affected, and sometimes throw stuff into the trash entirely. It was absolutely horrible. It was not baby spit. Not at all.

I gave up even trying to explain it to others. The minute I would start talking about it, I would get interrupted with, "Oh, I know just what you're talking about. My baby spit up all the time, too. One time I even had to bathe my child again and change the sheets. Benjamin will grow out of it, so be encouraged."

It was pure talent that kept me from yelling to tell them that they were misunderstanding the situation. I was baffled that I was never able to finish telling my vomiting dilemma. I can still feel the weight in the pit of my stomach when the realization hit me that I couldn't make people understand. I was alone in the vomiting business!

Now, I am not generally a bitter person. It is easy for me to see the best in people because I love life and I love people. But this experience of feeling like I was constantly left behind and misread was leaving me in a muddle.

After one such agonizing day I texted my dear mother to tell her I was having a terrible day on the special needs trail, and I shared how my heart was breaking from feeling so utterly misunderstood and alone. What could a mother say in response to a daughter in despair?

"Always forgive and always eat chocolate!"

I was so blessed by her response. Pity would have made me feel so much worse. Encouragement to forgive just knocked the socks off my tiny feet, and I was greatly honored and humbled to have wisdom so profound thrown at me at a very dark hour of my life. May I just say I have the most amazing mother in the history of ever!

Let me just unwrap this giant sized snickers chocolate bar. I am forty-six years old and my Mom said I could have it. Chomp!

ELEVEN

Mountaintops

"MOM, YOU GOT A PRETTY card in the mail!" Diana came rolling to a stop on her pink, banana bike, narrowly missing the daffodils just popping their bright yellow colors along the pea gravel path. "Here it is, Mom. I wonder who it could be from."

Laurie came dashing in behind her on the purple bicycle, even more scarcely avoiding the spring flowers and me as well. I felt the rushing wind from the narrow escape I just had from being unceremoniously mowed down.

"Hmm, let me see. Oh, awesome! It's a wedding invitation from my cousin a few hours away." *I guess we will have to miss it,* I thought to myself.

All afternoon I kept thinking about the wedding. The more I thought about it, the more I wanted to attend. Was it possible to go with Benjamin? So far we hadn't taken him anywhere other than to doctors' appointments and to church.

I showed the wedding invitation to Maynard when he came home, once he managed to disentangle himself from the host of little girlies clinging to his legs, arms, or shirttail.

"Vas dengsht?" I was speaking in our mother tongue, Pennsylvania Dutch, and asking Maynard what he thought. "Should we actually pack up our complicated little baby boy and go to the wedding?"

All I know is that we were both feeling youthful and energetic, because we decided right then and there that we would go to that wedding. It would take a lot of prepping and planning, but we couldn't stay home forever. We had been home from the hospital for four months now, and someday we would have to face all the blessed machines, and the obvious walking hospital we would be and just go do it.

So, because I never do anything halfway, we packed it all up and we hauled ourselves and our little hospital right smack dab into that wedding. We were equipped with a feeding pump on an IV pole attached to our stroller, a suction machine, a small bottle of oxygen and a pulse-oximeter to monitor his sat levels. It was our first time out and about where people were not familiar with Benjamin and his medical issues. Doctors and nurses knew all about Benny, of course, our family understood all about him, and our church family nary batted an eye when the suction machine whirred to life. The wedding guests? Not so much. Judging by the golf ball sized eyes that tried not to stare, it seemed that not one finely dressed guest had ever seen a trach before. Nobody was unkind or rude. In fact, they were overly polite. So polite, that they spoke very little to us. Not because they didn't want to, but because they didn't know what to say.

It became distinctly clear after only a few minutes of being there that we would ever and always be different; that odd family rolling into town while curious people line up to stare. One person after another came up to us, all smiles until they looked down into the stroller, then I saw pity wash over their face. They stammeringly excused themselves and awkwardly moved on to chat with someone else. I was done. The wedding hadn't even started yet but it felt impossible to bear the long evening. All I wanted to do was to leave the fastest way possible, hide my Benny from staring eyes, go home, and hide even myself. I would stay home forever, never to surface again.

I was on a slippery slope speeding straight into the formidable face of reality. The onslaught of raw emotions hit me squarely between my blue eyes, and stabbed my already broken heart. We had gone through so much the last few unbelievable months, accepting diagnostics and blunt truths as they came along one by one. I had never even thought about how it would be to go out in the general public, facing people whose fluffy yellow ducks were all lined up and even quacking in perfect harmonious quacks.

The great tidal wave of the real world racing towards me wanted to make me lose my already teetering balance, as it hit me full force in its unforgiving strength. It wanted to defeat me and wash me far, far away to the barren shores of Never Land. Parenting a child with disabilities would be hard and I felt like throwing in the unwieldy towel that night. But I didn't. I would never on God's green earth give up. Never. I would need to become a strong brave person.

The love for my sweet Benny compelled me to stand up on my quivering feet. No matter if the staring eyes grew to baseball sized proportions, I would always be by his side, fighting my way through it all, conquering any battle thrown in my overwhelming path. Being too weary is not an option, even though we do become exhausted.

That evening as we left the wedding, hauled our beeping hospital back to our trusty vehicle, and started home, I grieved. I mourned the loss of a healthy child we thought we would have. Deeply and intensely, it all came crashing down on me that night smothering me in its powerful grip. The stark reality, that the life we thought we would have was forever changed, hit me like a freight train and whisked me along on its quest across a vast, hot desert. The thick, black smoke from the chugging steam engine blinded and choked me so that I lost my vision for a time, making me feel utterly helpless. I cried out in frustration to God. I cried on Maynard's kind shoulder; he cried with me, and put his arm around me telling me it would all be okay. Then suddenly I stopped my sobbing and peace flooded my soul.

I lifted my head as the smoke cleared and the train came to a groaning, squealing halt. We were at the base of a massive mountain. I could sense this was a very important moment in time. I had a decision to make. I could get off this horrible train and climb that mountain, changing the destiny of my attitude, or I could stay on this train of overwhelming despair and wreck my life and the lives of all those around me. I only hesitated for a moment as I sped to my feet and leaped off that monstrous, black train. I had a difficult journey ahead of me, but I would scale the upcoming climb, and overcome the obstacles one at a time. The realization hit me that I would need much resolve, and to become many things through the process.

I would need to become *courageous*. When I would notice other children Benjamin's age easily mastering goals that he works years to accomplish, I would need to be gracious enough to smile and cheer them on as they race ahead.

I would need to become *resilient*. In my efforts to get all the assistance that I can for him to thrive, I would need to stand up to the insurance companies and the medical field. It would be an ongoing battle and extremely tiring.

I would need to exercise flexibility and grow a *healthy nervous system* that could stand the test of a public display of tears and screaming when Benjamin doesn't like the children lining up to stare and his eyes tell me, *"Make it stop, Mom!"* Or maybe

118

we would be at an event and he would be unable to process the noise. We might not be sure what is bothering him, but we need to be able to pack it up and leave immediately. Our vehicle would become a storm shelter more times than I could count.

I would need to learn to *walk graciously*. When I'm out in public, well meaning people often ask ignorant questions or make hurtful comments. *Did I rightly hear what they just said?* For example:

One day, Ellie and I decided to have a garage sale. I packed up my Benny and sat out to help. I wasn't able to stay long, because the heat was too much for Benjamin and I would have needed the oxygen bottle in order for him to tolerate the high temperatures. We stayed just long enough for one of the first customers to walk up to Benny and peer judgmentally at him.

"What are *his* issues?" the rudeness in the manner with which she spoke fried me right to a crisp like an egg on a hot sidewalk. I retaliated and did the unthinkable, and was rude right back. I just looked at her and refused to speak. She shrugged and walked away. It was not one of my gracious moments and I am not proud of my response, but this is why I was on the mountain hike. I had not yet learned to welcome these queries, and make them an opportunity to educate people.

I would need to become *compassionate*. Unless we get the chance to walk in another person's shoes, we can't fully understand what they are experiencing. I may know the small area of my own special needs world, but I don't know how to walk alongside a cancer patient. The ache of a broken heart and dreams I understand, though, and this is something that is probably associated with most illnesses and diseases, so I can reach out in the compassion that Jesus Christ freely gives.

I would need to be able to *laugh*. A generous *sense of humor* is needed when people ask how I know if he's crying when he can't make any vocal sounds because of his trach...

"Well let's see now. His face is all broken up and totally not smiling. There are torrents of tears running from his eyes. I can see his tonsils and count his teeth because his mouth is wide open while he's howling silently. There are whooshing noises coming from his trach. That is how I know he's crying," I explain, trying to keep a straight face, as I nimbly turn on the suction machine, to clear his airway. Only to have them ask in wide eyed amazement, "Oh! How often do you have to feed him through that thing on his neck?"

Fighting not to collapse in giggles, I continue to explain.

"The trach is an airway. I don't think his lungs would appreciate a dose of milk invading their privacy. He has a feeding tube into his stomach and we feed him through that around the clock."

Because we wouldn't have known these details either, had we not been thrown into this medical world, we had to learn not to laugh out loud in front of the person asking the questions. But it sure did us good to laugh about it later.

I would need to become completely *unselfish*. This would enter into all aspects of life. Just like when you have a baby. They can't do a single thing for themselves, not even get out of bed, bathe, or feed themselves. And so it was with our special needs child.

We do every single thing for Benny. At exactly 5:30am we get him up and give him a bath. We do it at this time of the morning because he insists on it. We do not yet smile at this hour. Well, I mean *I* don't smile. Maynard has the insane ability to smile like a cat at any moment. Benny is ecstatic to be up and delighted to begin his day. We change his diaper many times during the day, feed him through his feeding tube, suction his trach, wipe his tears, rescue him from many mischievous acts, play music for him, sing for him, wipe his puke messes, bathe him at least one more time, and when the long day is ended, the nights begin. We get up about ten to twelve times a night to suction. When he has even a slight cold, we get up much more often than twelve times. Benjamin's needs come before our needs every time. He will never grow out of it.

We, as a family, would need to *bear the special needs cross* with Benny. One day, on this grand mountain climb, just before I reached the peak of the mountain, I encountered the toughest obstacle of all. I don't even know what word to use to describe it other than bearing Benny's cross. Acceptance? Yes, acceptance that we have become a special needs family. It was inevitable and I knew we would face this ultimate test someday.

"Mom, Dad! Roger just said that Benjamin is a retard. Is he?" Diana sounded troubled as she announced this bombshell onto the unsuspecting ears of us as a family.

We were all in the van, on our way home from a summer picnic which was complete with cold chicken legs and homemade root beer. The shocked hush that followed was so thick and foggy, I could scarcely breathe.

I looked over at Maynard, my patient, good hearted man, and hoped he had the answers.

"Girls, come up front so you can all hear." Maynard stepped in to explain. "First, we don't use the word retard. Ever. And nobody else should either. You all know Benjamin is not like other children, right? He will not ever be like other children. Back in the day, people called these children retarded. Today we call kids like Benjamin *special needs*. Benjamin is a special needs child, but we love him just the same as if he was as healthy as all of you beautiful girls."

"Yeah," exclaimed Laurie furiously. "No one should say Benjamin is retarded. He is special. And cute. And sweet. And I love him so much."

I heard her young voice crack with emotion, and just like that we had a van full of four crying girls. Thankfully, my amazing husband grew up the only boy with six sisters, making him the perfect father who could understand a houseful of female emotions. With many loving hugs and assurances, he comforted his princesses until they were okay.

When you stop and listen to conversations, or when you have your own special needs child, you hear this word everywhere. It has become like an insulting slang word. People call each other retards all the time. I have even heard parents calling their perfectly normal children this. Usually in Wal-Mart. And the low class person committing this heinous crime is most certainly wearing sweatpants or leggings filled out to overstretched proportions, not meant for any decent eyes to see, from years of French fries and soda pop intake. The sweat rushing from my armpits rivals Niagara Falls as I almost faint from blistering said person with my opinion, as I quickly walk away.

I once overheard someone say the streets of Pittsburgh are retarded. Hmm. That's a good one. One time I overheard a beautiful, Godly girl calling herself retarded! What?

Recently someone told us our dog is so retarded. Granted, he is a mite strange. He barks at his own humans coming home from work. He hides under the furniture whenever his favorite human leaves the house, and he has the misfortune of resembling a wet rat.

Although it is meant as an offhand remark, to us as special needs family units, it is like an arrow piercing our soul.

When our family members hear the "R" word, we become saber toothed tigers. We get fangs and claws and anything else needed to protect our dear Benjamin. Our insides curl, and we literally can't ever forget the person that used the word. Not that we dislike the person or feel bitterness towards them; we just remember. Like giant gray elephants with an endless memory tank.

Then, one day, even closer to the mountain peak, Maynard casually shared with one of his friends this episode of the girls hearing the "R" word for the first time, in reference to Benny.

"I have noticed you seem troubled lately, Maynard. Is something wrong?" inquired Billy, sipping his cup of coffee casually.

"No, we are just working through things as a family. The girls learned that their friends are saying Benny is a retard, and we are working through it. It is painful to hear it for the first time, but we will be okay." answered Maynard.

"Maynard, it is time you and Marietta accept that Benjamin is not normal."

Billy seemed disgusted that we were even hurt by the fact that someone called Benjamin retarded.

"What are you talking about? We know he's not like other children." Maynard couldn't keep the anguish from his voice.

"It seems like you aren't accepting things for what they are. Benjamin *is* "retarded". I know people don't call it that anymore so I see what you're saying, but he is not like other children. You have to accept it and go on." Billy continued.

"Yes, we do have to accept it. I guess I thought we had, but maybe to other people it appears like we haven't." Maynard spoke in soft, defeated tones.

After all the diagnostics and days of acceptance, we had been through. After it was revealed and settled in our hearts that we indeed would be a special needs family, why were we so misunderstood?

I have never shared with anyone before this, how humiliated and ashamed that conversation made me feel. I felt like a naughty child caught passing a love note in school. The shame caused me to hang my head. For a long, long time I allowed myself to feel condemned. Even today I have a hard time putting it into words in a way that you might understand.

After that, because of the bitterness I allowed in my heart, the mountain climb became intensely difficult, and it seemed I slid into a deep ravine and got lodged in the brambles and bushes. To be so accused stung like a hive of angry bees had attacked me. I can still feel the prick of betrayal that came with that statement, and the condescending tone in with which it was delivered.

I wrestled with my pain a good long time on the mountain, trying to make sense of something so bizarre. I tried barreling through the thorns without taking the time to heal from the intense burden of broken relationships and rejection established through our hospital stay. My wounds only became deeper as I fought to escape without healing first from the bitterness I had allowed to creep inside my heart. As the storms raged around us, I felt a chilly bit of ice forming around my soul.

"Why must this special needs hike be so difficult?" I lamented to God in despair. "Why are we so hard to understand? We are just trying to raise our family for you! Do you even hear our prayers?"

I glanced over at Benny. He was a little child so precious and sweet, who knew nothing but love and goodness. Why should I carry around a load of anger and resentment when I had a tiny boy as pure as snow? This lad deserved a mother with a free spirit unhindered by bitterness or wrath.

I was stricken with remorse, as I allowed my gaze to rest on God. I dreaded the fact that I would have to face God's own pain and suffering in order for his healing love to flow through me and cleanse me. I sensed his hand on my shoulder assuring me of his healing and forgiveness that would then set me free to forgive others. I grasped his hand tightly, praying for strength, understanding and grace.

Suddenly as I surrendered all the pain, anger and bitterness to God, the storms gave way to giant waterfalls flowing out of massive rocks. The birds became alive, singing their songs and the flowers bloomed in vibrant colors. I inhaled this breath of fresh air like it was a life saving oxygen. I was free from ill feelings and bitterness at last!

And so it came to pass on a bright sunny morning we joyfully crested the mountain peak, thankful to have accomplished this great feat. As we looked out over the wide expanse, our eyes were met by green pastures and lilies blooming by the way, but we also noticed more mountain ridges! The realization hit us that although we had achieved an amazing climb, there would be more harrowing summits ahead. There would be times of rest and tranquility in the lush valleys, but then we would need to climb again for more wisdom and knowledge. We felt the presence of God, his warm hand on our shoulder welcoming us on the journey and assuring us that all mountain paths will lead us home. We knew all would be well as long as we walked in stride with our trail guide, the God of heaven and earth. We looked at each other, sighed long, fulfilled sighs, gathered up our Benny and our precious daughters, and turned to face the sun. Marching on...!

TWELVE

Heart Surgery and Miracles

"HEY, WHAT ARE YOU doing back here?" exclaimed Nancy, hugging the breath out of us before diving towards Benny. "Bobo, it's so good to see you, my handsome little man! Do you have any idea how unusual it is that you stayed out of the hospital for a whole year?"

"We have been pretty fortunate," we answered cheerily. "Benjamin developed pneumonia. We tried everything we could, but couldn't keep his sat levels up so we brought him in. They said we should be able to go home in a few days."

"That's good, and we will love him to bits while he's here. Ashley! Benny is here!" yelled Nancy poking her head out the door and hollering down the hall, causing Ashley to turn around to descend on Benjamin and smooch him to smithereens.

"I will alert all his doctors that he is here. Maybe they can all have a look and update anything that needs done or scheduled," announced the house doctor.

While we were waiting, the girls enjoyed being back at Rainbow, receiving all manner of Popsicles from the staff, and sipping water from the drinking fountains.

"Oh! A drinking fountain," blurted Hannah, "I saw it first!"

This caused a stampede of four girls to hammer it to see who could get there first. Why must there be one around every hospital corner? Just sitting there, a small one and a larger one, along the wall in all their stainless steel glory, waiting to see if moms across the universe have any patience in their storehouses of parenting abilities. I had a spur of the moment insanity come over me, and I decided to make drinking fountains fun instead of a thorn in my side. I checked to make sure there was no one in sight, and then I sprung into action.

"Oh! I will race you!" My words came out in breathless bursts. "I'm gonna beat you!"

All four girls halted in their tracks to look at me, as I sailed right by them and beat them to the drinking fountain.

"Beat ya! And I am so thirsty, too." I raved, slurping water like a thirsty little yapping dog.

They were right on my heels, giggling and carrying on, trying to pull me away from *their* drinking fountain.

We had a visit from each of Benny's physicians. The trach doctor examined Benjamin, and informed us his jaw was nowhere near ready for the trach to be removed. We had not been anticipating removal of the trach anyway, so we weren't surprised.

The bone doctor examined him and gave him a clean bill of health from scoliosis.

The GI doctor scheduled a Gastric Emptying Scan to see if his stomach was emptying correctly. Benny's vomiting was getting out of control.

We got both good news and bad news from the Cardiologist. Benny's ASD closed up all by itself. But the VSD was causing problems. We had not expected this at all, and we felt pretty devastated about it. They wanted to schedule surgery as soon as possible. The biggest concern was his recovery time, and the doctors warned us that it could get nasty.

We were discharged without incident, with Benjamin's heart surgery scheduled for April 12.

"Hey, Maynard, remember that healing CD that lady had given me when we stayed at the Ronald McDonald house? I forgot all about it, but I'm going to search for it. I know I have it somewhere. She said it would heal Benny's heart to have healing songs running in the background. Let's play that CD as much as we can. She said it doesn't have to be loud, just playing quietly," I announced hopefully. We found this CD, and started playing it softly throughout each day. Sometimes I even put it on at night. It was calming and peaceful.

"Mom, may I stop the healing CD and put another one on?" asked Hannah.

"Sure, Hannah, when you are done, be sure to put the healing one back in though." I replied. "What are you going to listen to?"

"I'm going to put the one in where the men sing about the underwear." she quipped. "Why would they sing that anyway? That's bad, isn't it? Why do we listen to it if it's bad?"

"What are you talking about? What song?" I was completely flabbergasted.

She showed me which song.

"I'll rest at the top of the stairs? That's the underwear line?" I implored, the hilarity of it was starting to tickle me all manner of pink. Hannah nodded.

"They don't say underwear, Hannah, they say, "top of the stair," I instructed.

"Oh." she answered quietly as it dawned on her how utterly mistaken she had been.

I heard snickers behind me as Diana and Laurie grasped what had just happened.

"Don't feel bad, Hannah. For the longest time I thought the line *He takes a beggar and makes him a king* was *He takes a beggar and makes him a pig!*" hooted Diana jovially.

We all had a good laugh at each other's expense.

By the next week I was beginning to feel the pressure of the impending trip back to Rainbow Babies Hospital.

"Okay, girls, we need to have your school done by April 12, so we won't have to worry about it when Benny has his surgery."

"Ugh, Mom, that doesn't sound like fun," complained Laurie. "I can suction Benny today so you can teach the others." I put my hands on my hips and gave her a look. She scowled and quickly picked up her pencil.

"Well, no matter if it's fun or not, we must do it anyway," I replied firmly.

I noticed that the girls were having a hard time concentrating and that they had a hefty dose of PDD. Pencil Dropsy Disease.

"Hey, if you drop your pencil one more time I will tie you to your chair like they do in Little House on the Prairie!" I threatened with a twinkle in my eye. It was a frustrated twinkle though, so I'm not sure how sparkly it was.

All four girls bust out in hilarious fits of giggles. I caught Hannah just as she sneaked behind Diana with a blanket, trying to quickly tie her leg to her chair, which started a whole myriad of chasing and dancing to escape each other.

With a house of girls, this is what happens! I remember it well from being at home with my four sisters. If Dad tried to scold us at the supper table it was unbearably funny. We would almost cry from trying so hard not to explode in uproarious laughter. It was impossible. One pair of eyes would accidentally meet the other pair across the table laden with meatloaf and potatoes, and we were off into uncontrollable gales of chortles and snorts. My dad had a lot of grace in this area, and usually just sighed and smiled a little bit after seeing there wasn't a thing he could do to stop it.

By this time Benny was going through a phase where he refused to take anything by mouth. He had strong opinions about this thing called food. His theory was to avoid anything resembling grub, and gag until he threw up every time some adventurous individual decided it would be a good idea to attempt to put something in his mouth again. This was pretty often. Until we made a family law.

"Remember the rule, Maynard! If you insert food in Benny's mouth, you wipe up the puke mess." I chided, watching as a grinning Maynard slyly hid the spoon of buttery mashed potatoes. He then made a loud whacking noise on the table to make Benny laugh, and took the open mouth opportunity to land that spoon of fluffy, smashed Idahoes right into the unsuspecting mouth of Benny.

"Look at his face!" giggled Diana. "He looks so grossed out, but he's not throwing up. Oops, here it comes! Oh, no, he only gagged this time! Dad, you offended him, he's going to cry. Aw, Benny, you poor little boy, come to Diana."

"Hey, there's an accomplishment. Maybe we are getting somewhere since that's the first time he hasn't thrown it all back up." I speculated with hope resounding throughout the kitchen table as Diana rescued Benny from another spoon episode.

We fell into some semblance of normality as best we could. We learned to avoid sickness at all costs. Benny got every little illness he was exposed to. Whether it was viral or bacterial, it landed faithfully in his already compromised respiratory system immediately. This meant misery for Benny and no sleep for us. He coughed all the time. It required suctioning and albuteral breathing treatments around the clock.

We determined to stay home from the hospital as long as we

130

could. We had our own stethoscope and we knew how to listen to lung sounds. We could tell when it was only in his bronchial tubes, or if it had reached his lungs. We watched all his monitors carefully and when it became obvious it was out of our expertise we would take him to the hospital where he was placed on the ventilator to help him along. Usually he had pneumonia or adenovirus, and almost always there was a collapsed lung involved too.

"Maynard, I was looking back over our last two years," I began.

"Yes?" queried Maynard.

"You sure you want to hear this? Do you realize we have barely slept for two whole entire years now?" I asked incredulously, grabbing my purse to go get groceries.

"True. I'm not sure how it's possible, but here we are. And Benny is sick yet again, so quickly go get groceries in case he gets worse," said Maynard with a visible worried stress line on his brow.

A shriek from the bathroom almost stopped my heart. It was one of those yelps when a mother is sure one of her child's limbs is dangling only by a thread. After the blood quit rushing through my skull, I knew exactly what it was.

"Mom!" wailed Samantha in pure and absolute terror. I could hear her stomping and soaking the whole bathroom down in her valiant efforts to dodge the hair floating in her bath water. "There's a hair in my bath. Help me! Mom, come, hurry!"

"You just told me to go get groceries, right? Okay, here I go, being the submissive little wife. I will let you be the hair killing super hero this time. Bye!" I laughed and sailed out the door before Maynard could come up with a retort. *Samantha is four years old, she will grow out of her hair floating phobia someday, but it sure is funny*, I thought as I backed the lumbering van out the gravel driveway.

I never made it to the first store.

"Yes?" I picked up the phone as I pulled into the grocery store parking lot.

"Come home, Benny suddenly turned worse. I can't get his SATS up and I think the breath sounds in his one lung are diminished," said Maynard urgently.

I rushed back home. *How did he get worse so quickly? He wasn't even that bad when I left.*

We found ourselves admitted to the PICU again, and sure enough a lung was collapsed.

"I'm sure it's no surprise to you that we need to cancel his heart surgery. Benny has been too sick and it's too risky. We will put it out another month and see how he is by that time." informed the cardiologist apologetically. "We need to get him well though, because these repeated sicknesses are because of his heart condition. I think once his heart is repaired, he will be much stronger and able to fight off these lung infections. He has so much against him, but he is a fighter that's for sure."

"Yes we understand," we answered wearily.

We were finally discharged after four days, hoping for no more episodes before his new surgery date, May 10.

Because we could hardly go anywhere without Benny getting sick, we learned to find other things to do for family fun. Sometimes we loaded up a picnic into our van and headed for a lake and just sat there by the water inside the van with our picnic. We had picnics as a family out on the trampoline. Every once in a while I took the girls to the library.

"Girls, let's go to the library today. I will stay outside in the van with Benny and you can have an hour of browsing time." I announced.

"Yay! The library! I will go start the van. Hannah, do you want to come with me?" asked Laurie eagerly.

They both raced out to the van, only to come running back

inside right away.

"Mom, remember this morning you told me the van door was open and you sent me to shut it?" gasped Hannah with a panicked look on her face.

"Yes, I recall." I answered, puzzled as to what could be wrong.

"Rufus is sitting right on the front seat! He must have been inside when I shut the door! Mom, I'm too scared he will bite me to open the door. Why does that dog have to be such a meaner? Now we can't go to the library!" wailed Hannah in despair.

They were right on the mark. I was even too scared to chase that little mean dog out of the van. He would surely eat us all alive. Even if he was only ten inches tall, he had a mean streak unparalleled to any tiny dog species I have ever witnessed.

"Okay, everyone be ready to load up, and I will see if I can lure him out with these hot dogs." *Whoa, where did that brave voice come from?* I wondered as I heroically stepped out with wieners from the fridge, and gingerly opened the van door. I walked away very casually with my shoulders thrown back and my nose way up in the air like Anne of Green Gables. With my heart nearly pounding out of my chest, and feeling the flush of embarrassment that I should allow myself to be afraid of a dog so small, I quickly deposited the hot dogs about 20 feet away. Rufus, the biting dog, eagerly followed my lead as the girls scurried silently into the van in the background. I joined them with an effortless leap into the driver's seat, and we got to go to the library after all.

That evening, as we told Maynard of our near death experience, he almost quit breathing from laughing so hard. We all laughed with him, threatening to whack him back to life like the rubber dolls. We were still feeling the heat of shame to be controlled by such a small but ferocious animal.

May 10th was coming closer and the dreaded surgery was looking us square in the eye.

"I would like to have our closest church friends, maybe four couples, come and have special prayer and an anointing of oil in the name of Jesus for Benny's heart. Would it be too much for you to prepare a snack and brew some coffee and have them over for the evening?" queried Maynard.

"Yes, I think we should. Would it be rude to ask them not to bring their children just in case one would be sick?" I asked apprehensively.

"No, that wouldn't be rude at all." answered Maynard. "That is common sense. Let me call and see when they can come. Would tonight work for us?"

I nodded, "I don't know why not. Call them and see if they can come."

I immediately began planning. "Diana, would you stir up a pan of cookie bars? It works for the couples to come tonight so we need to get the house picked up, too. Laurie and Hannah, you can do that. I need a volunteer to keep the coffee brewed and served then while they are here."

"I will do that," offered Laurie kindly.

"Here, Sam, you can Windex the two front doors!" I smiled and handed her the Windex bottle and a roll of paper towels.

Sam joyously grabbed her equipment and eagerly completed her chore. With tongue clenched between her teeth in avid concentration, she vigorously applied Windex, like only a four year old can. A lot of it, and with streaks still running down the panels even after she was done.

That evening was a special time as we all circled around Benny, praying for a miracle and anointing him with a few drops of olive oil in the name of Jesus. We experienced a peace coming down over the room, and we believed that God would heal him.

Four days before his surgery, Benjamin came down with a terrible fever, but he got over it without a lung infection. We packed up our bags and headed with angst towards the hospital, praying for our miracle of healing to be made known in the last hour. When we arrived, and were put in our room, we noticed a faint rash all over his body seemingly just under his skin. The prep nurses were in and out all throughout the day, and then cardiology came to take him for an ultra sound.

Benjamin's rash had become noticeably angry and red as the hours went on.

"Whoa, what is this?" they exclaimed. "Benjamin has a rash all over his body. We are sorry but we will probably have to cancel the surgery."

The head of cardiology came in quickly after being summoned.

"Mr. and Mrs. Troyer, we cannot put Benny under surgery with anything like this rash present. Although it is probably a result from the fevers he had last week, there is still something going on somewhere. Open-heart surgery is too serious to risk it. I am so sorry for the time you already spent here, but I will have to reschedule. You can go home, and we will call with another date."

We walked out of the hospital, both relieved and mystified. What was God up to? Benjamin wasn't healed, but surgery was now canceled the second time. Honestly, we didn't know what to think, so we just trusted.

We went home and waited for the call to let us know when the next surgery was scheduled. It came two days later, informing us of the next date which would be July 12.

By this time Benny had learned to sit all by himself. He was two years of age. We were thrilled and he looked so cute sitting on the floor playing with his toys.

"Look, Mom, I taught Benny hi-five!" beamed Sammy. "Hi-five, Benny?"

Benny perked right up and gave her a hi-five. We couldn't even get over it. He was learning things! Had he just won a gold medal at the Olympics, we wouldn't have been any prouder. And so the teaching from four older sisters began.

"Twiddle your thumbs, Benny!" He twiddled his thumbs.

"Scratch your head, Benny?" Benny leaned his head forward for us to scratch.

"Clap your hands, Benny." He clapped his hands.

"Wave your foot, Benny!" He shot his leg up in the air and waved his foot and only his foot. His leg didn't move one inch as he swiveled that little foot back and forth at the ankles.

"Hey, Benny, how do you do?" He put his hand out to shake our hands.

We went a little crazy. The funniest was showing him the box of the hair-cutting machine we had.

"Benny, want a haircut?" Then we would shove the box under his nose so he could have a good look. And Benny would make the saddest poochy mouth in the world and sometimes he even cried. A haircut was the thing nightmares were made of according to Benny.

He learned he could make a sound with his trach if he tucked his chin down over it and puffed air through it. It sounded a little bit like a whale snorting in the ocean. He was so proud to be able to make that one vocal sound, and of course we laughed and clapped whenever he did it, which caused him to thrill at showing off for us.

We kept believing in that miracle of healing even as we made another trip to the hospital on July 11th to prep for surgery.

"Benny, let's get you down for one last ultra sound to get one more look before tomorrow," smiled the orderly as he wheeled Benny down the hall. We walked alongside him, as we headed to radiology.

"Wait right here while I get the cardiologist," said the nurse hastily as she went to call the doctor in.

We watched them carefully through the window as the doctor and the radiologist both looked and looked again. Finally the doctor stepped out and said through tears, "I can't explain this, but his VSD is almost closed up! Not completely, but it is definitely forming tissue, and closing up by itself. I have no way to explain it except that it is a miracle. There is no need for surgery! Are you a praying family?"

We nodded. We remained speechless as tears rolled down our cheeks at this revelation of healing. The cardiologist cried happy tears as he hugged us and told us we could go home.

"If I would have wanted this to happen to anyone it is Benny. He has been through so much, and I was very fearful of his recovery time from surgery. Now run off to home, and don't come back for a long time!"

We had just experienced a miracle straight from heaven! Three times Benny had been scheduled for surgery. Twice he got so sick we had to cancel. It didn't feel like a miracle during the cancellations. It didn't seem like God was moving any mountains, or that he was parting the waters for us to walk through. It felt like setbacks in a battle we could not win. We were so impatient and disheartened.

God was watching and reminding us during those times to be patient and wait on him. He was at work healing Benny's heart. Only he knew how much time was needed.

We smiled at the doctor, a smile loaded with all the sorrows from the past and now the joy of the moment.

In the end we had the miracle we had prayed for. We were so humbled and elated! God's plans are always good!

THIRTEEN
Lung Surgery

"DAD, WHY WOULD GOD send children out to war? I mean, that's just not right," stated Samantha.

We had been going through the Old Testament for family devotions and God was sending the "children of Israel" here and there to war.

"Sam, that's a good question, but the children of Israel refers to a whole group of adult people, not children," clarified Maynard.

"Oh, that's good," sighed Sammy, "I was getting worried!"

"You don't need to worry anymore. You better get your schoolwork started and I better get to work," Maynard said, looking up as I walked in with a coughing, wheezing, feverish Benny.

"Oh, no," I announced, dread dripping from every pore. "Benny is sick again. Let's set up a nurse's station, girls. We will need the oxygen, pulse-oximeter, nebulizer, suction, mist machine, feed pump and electrolytes, and temperature glass all right here at hand. Oh, grab the stethoscope and bagger, too."

"Got it, Mom," answered the girls, going about the task of getting everything set up like we always did when Benny got sick, in hopes of staying out of the hospital and fighting the battle to wellness at home. Benny was three years old by now, and we had been having good success lately with this. We found that if we immediately started breathing treatments and bagged him to get the gunky stuff loose from inside his lungs; we could often be triumphant in our efforts to keep him home.

Unfortunately, we almost waited too long this time. Benny had an awful case of pneumonia by the time we took him to the doctor's office.

"How long has he been breathing this hard?" asked his doctor, concern lacing her voice.

"I think the last twenty-four hours he has gotten worse pretty fast," Maynard answered.

"Okay, well he needs admitted immediately. He is worse than I thought he would be. When I told you two days ago that you should stay home, I didn't realize it was quite this bad," she said apologetically. "I should have seen him before advising you like that. I am sorry. He is in pretty bad shape. Let's get him over to the hospital right away."

I had a heavy feeling in the pit of my stomach as we walked across the parking lot to the hospital.

"Benny's here! Oh, no, he's sick again? We will get him brand new in no time, Mom." Carrie, one of the good nurses, squeezed my hand as we made ourselves comfortable and started the paperwork.

"Look, my main fear of being in the hospital is the respiratory therapists and nurses not listening when I say to not suction past five centimeters. The marks are right on the catheter, and unless they are deep suctioning specifically, there is no reason to go down any further than the bottom of the trach. Benny will throw up every single time." Tiredness and angst were all coming through loud and clear as I voiced my apprehension to Patty, our night nurse.

"Let me fix that for you," she smiled. "I will be right back."

Moments later she was back with tape and a sign. She taped it right onto Benny's headboard in bold black letters. On bright white paper were these words: DO NOT EVER SUCTION PAST 5 CENTIMETERS. THANK YOU!

"Well, thanks, Patty. That is perfect!" I laughed and felt assured that no one would dare suction past the stated mark after that.

Never underestimate the young, barely out of school therapist who is taught to do everything by the book. I watched her warily and got this feeling that crept up my mother spine, alerting me that an episode may or may not be about to happen, and that I should be on my guard.

"Be sure not to suction past five centimeters. He throws up if you do." I warned.

Young, trained by the book nurse looked at me, smiled as if to say, *and what does a little lady like you know about suctioning*, and dove right past the five and just kept going. I leaped out of my chair as the vomit shot out of Benny's mouth so fast we had no chance to avoid trach ties, trach mask, corrugated tubing, and all bedding in close vicinity to be affected. I had it up to my eyeballs right then and there.

My voice came out in first high-pitched shrieks then reverted to dangerously ominous lows, "I told you to not suction past the five! It's right on the catheter! Did you even look? Now look at the mess we have. He probably aspirated some into his lungs, making his pneumonia worse!" I was so upset that tears ran down my face, mostly in anger, I admit, but none the less, tears.

"What's going on in here," inquired Patty taking in the scene.

"I told her not to suction past the trach, five centimeters, and she did anyway," I blurted.

"Mrs. Troyer, I am so sorry. I am so, so sorry. You did tell me, and I didn't listen. Please forgive me. I will help you with all the clean up, and get new trach ties and everything," she apologized and was almost crying herself.

Now I felt really terrible. What bad manners I had! Never in my life, under normal circumstances would I even think to speak to another person this way. *What has happened to me?* I asked myself, disheartened. *What have I become?*

"Of course I forgive you," I assured her. "Let's get this mess cleaned up."

Poor Benny, so sick and then a senseless suction induced vomiting episode. I could hardly bear it as we cleaned everything right down to changing his trach ties. I'm not sure how it happened, but I looked down and suddenly realized that his entire trach was out.

"Oh, his trach is out," I said, reaching across the bed to put it back in, but he was just out of my reach.

I nearly jumped out of my skin when the nurse yelled at the top of her lungs, as she ran towards the door, "Trach is out!" And just like that a stampede of doctors and nurses were coming down the hall running.

Now I don't say this to brag at my lightening quick reflexes or anything vain like that, but I have reflexes that could win an Olympic gold medal. I'm astonishingly fast at popping a trach back in. Without thinking, I had the trach back in before the stampede ever reached Benny's bedside. I was almost embarrassed for the nurse that had yelled so frantically and caused such a panic.

If I have learned one thing through doing trach care, it is that nurses in general are scared of trachs. Hence is the fear to begin with when I mentioned to Patty about the now famous five centimeter mark. I had been in hospitals enough to figure this out, and it was an insecure feeling. But they better listen to

Mom and Dad, because we do it every day and we know how. A good nurse would carefully ask us what worked for Benny and she would go with it.

"Oh, you already put the trach back in," she smiled graciously, not able to keep the flush of red from creeping up her neck. "Whew, you're fast!"

I nodded, then went back to clean up. *What does the little lady know now? Hmm?* I thought to myself smugly.

After two days, Benny did not get better. He was definitely worse.

"Okay, time to get out the ventilator. I thought we could go without it this time, but his pneumonia is getting worse and not better. He is putting too much energy into breathing. Let's get this hooked up and see if a break from the hard work of breathing will help him improve," instructed the PICU house doctor.

After watching his labored breathing for the last couple of days, it was a great relief to finally see the ventilator doing some of the breathing for him.

All packaged up with IV's and ART lines, Benjamin looked like a little boxing champion. He sported bright, green, neon gloves on each fist and even on both feet.

Throughout the long, agonizing weekend, the vent alarms constantly went off with ear splitting squeals. It kept the nurses running.

"You know, I think he has figured out that the vent kicks in and breathes for him when he gets too tired. He is one exhausted, sick little boy. I'm going to ask if we should just change the settings where it does all the breathing for him without him activating it by not breathing. Oh, Benny, my baby darling, you are so sick." Carrie crooned. The sadness in her voice carried over into my heart, causing tears to run down my cheeks.

The PICU doctor signed the order to this setting. It eased

the constant terror of the vent alarms going off to notify us of no air moving through his lungs, then kicking in to do it for him until he picked up and did it by himself again.

"Good morning, Mrs. Troyer. We are ready to do rounds. You are welcome to sit with us and listen in," Dr. Miller said, popping his head into the room.

"Okay, thank you!" I answered readily. I always eavesdropped anyway, so I may as well sit in on it without sneaking when the opportunity presented itself.

"Benjamin is three years old. He has been in PICU for five days. He has a bad case of pneumonia. We can usually snap him out of it within about two days, but this time he is taking longer to recover and get well. The plan is to keep doing what we are and we are confident he will get well." He paused to smile kindly in my direction. "Does anyone have any questions?"

The team of doctors voiced a few inquiries and they discussed more options and gave some suggestions then shook my hand and moved on. I was always impressed with their good manners, and the impression they gave of really caring.

This hospital was in Youngstown and only twenty minutes from home. The Rainbow Babies doctors were running the PICU, which is the only reason we agreed to this medical facility. We were familiar with all the doctors we had on Benjamin's case. They had all cared for him at Cleveland. So handy and we could take turns to stay with Benny so one of us could go home each night to rest.

We did this until Benjamin got so bad that I couldn't bear to be there alone at night with him. One night as I left, I couldn't shake the feeling that Benny would die that night.

"He's going to die tonight, honey. I just know it. Look at him, Maynard. He looks like he's already gone. He hasn't even moved for the last hour and his color is unlike any I have ever seen. He looks gray. Doesn't he look gray, Maynard?" I sobbed, "He's dying, isn't he?"

"Honey, I don't know. Just go home. Go home and rest and I will call you right away if anything goes wrong, okay?" persuaded Maynard bravely.

"No, I am not going home until you get the doctor in here to ask if Benny is dying," I replied stubbornly.

Moments later the doctor came in, listening as Maynard explained that we felt like Benny is likely in his last hours.

"I can't tell you one way or the other right now. He is bad. He could die during the night, or he could turn around and get better tonight. We won't know until the morning and we will see how things are by then." Compassion and sadness came through his voice as he reached out to give us both a big hug.

"If you are praying people, now would be a good time to pray," he advised.

I went home that night, so distraught I could not even pray. I felt the prayers of others, though, and I was peaceful enough to fall into a fitful slumber.

The jingling of the phone woke me early the next morning. With great dread and a trembling voice, I picked up the phone.

"Marietta, it's me, Maynard. Hey, just wanted to say Benny seems a little more alert, but they found out during the night that he has fluid in his lungs. They aren't sure why, so he will be going into emergency surgery real soon. If you want to see him before they take him, you should come right away."

"Okay, I will be there within an hour," I said, scrambling around to gather everything we needed. I then called our pastor to start a prayer hotline, and hugged the girls before I dashed out the door.

I rushed up to Benny's room. He was so tiny and lying so still. "Benny, my baby, I love you so much," I whispered, my heart shattering into a million pieces. He opened his eyes at the sound of my voice and gave me a weak smile.

Our pastor, Eldon, soon arrived. We were so glad to see him, and to have someone with us during this time.

Then Dr. Nason walked in, one of our favorite doctors from Rainbow.

"I have one question, Dr. Nason, with all respect; please tell me honestly if this surgeon is good. Because if you have the slightest doubt, we want him transferred to Cleveland." I said apprehensively.

"That is a good question, but you have nothing to fear. Dr. Alloy is one of the best." she answered confidently.

Soon they came and took our little Benny away. We said goodbye to him with great fear and trembling, leaving it in the Father's hands to guide the doctors hands. They assured us it would only be an hour or so. When we got to the waiting room, Mervin Shrocks and my parents were also there to sit with us. We were so thankful to have them with us when the hour turned to two hours, then crept as slow as molasses to three hours.

Finally the doctor burst through the doors, smiling and reaching out to shake our hands, "Troyers, I am so sorry, it took much longer than anticipated. It was by far the worst case of pneumonia I have ever seen. It was so bad that it had eaten a hole through his lung, causing part of his lung to decay. His ½ inch incision turned into a six inch incision because we had to go to his rib cage, remove a muscle flap, and stitch it onto his lung for a patch."

We were speechless. He had patched Benny's lung with a muscle flap from Benny's own rib cage? How is that even possible, and how does that work as he grows? I couldn't fathom it right then, so the questions all had to wait for another day. One thing I knew. The right surgeon was there that night. Other doctors since have told us that they hope we understand what an incredible job this surgeon did, and had it been any other, the outcome would not have been a happy one. He had to make a quick decision as he opened up Benny and was confronted with something way unexpected. It was a good reminder that Benny has a divine purpose in life.

The surgeon continued, "He has three chest tubes to drain fluids. We will keep them in for a few days, and then slowly take one at a time off over a period of days. Oh, there he goes. You may follow him up to his room if you want."

Eldon and Mervins quickly said goodbye as my parents and Maynard and I scurried along behind Benny's gurney.

"Mom!" I gasped. "Look at Benjamin. He looks just like an angel, doesn't he?"

My mom nodded, "Yes, he does. He is an angel child, that's why."

His stark white face was framed by a halo of black hair. He no longer struggled to breath and his facial muscles were totally relaxed. There was such an expression of complete innocence on his pure, beautiful, little face that I couldn't tear my eyes away. He was so precious and dear.

It was a long hard road to recovery with many painful set-backs. The doctors were at their wit's end when Benny's stomach kept bloating a few days after surgery. Thankfully with his feeding tube it was easy to vent the buildup of air that caused great swelling and discomfort.

Finally Maynard couldn't keep quiet anymore, "It's because of his cuffed trach. He doesn't have one normally. You put one in to seal the ventilator leaks, which worked great while he was on the vent. But he is breathing on his own now, and isn't used to a cuffed trach, so he swallows the air because he doesn't know what to do with it. Well, anyway that's what my 8th grade edu-cated brain tells me," offered Maynard.

146

Patty looked at him in surprise, "That actually makes sense, Mr. Troyer! I'm going to ask the doctor right now."

A little while later the doctor walked in just as Maynard was venting Benny's stomach for the fourth time that hour.

"You think it's because of his cuffed trach, Mr. Troyer? I mean, I've never heard of this happening before, ever. But it could make sense. Why not give it a try? If you're right, you're hired, Mr. Troyer!" laughed the doctor.

"Oh, I am right," answered Maynard with a mischievous grin. "Bring the new trach. I will even put it in for you."

"One of the nurses can do it for you," countered the doctor.

"No reason for them to do it. We do it all the time. No offense meant, but I'm better at it than they are," teased Maynard, winking slyly at Patty.

"Hey!" retorted Patty. "But I agree that it's true. You guys have this trach thing down to an art."

Maynard popped the new trach in and we waited for the stomach to bloat...waited...waited...and today we are still waiting because it never happened again.

"That's it, Mr. Troyer. You're hired. When can you start?" joked the doctor as he slapped Maynard on the back. "Great job, man. We were totally baffled."

A week later, after the chest tubes were successfully removed, and we were thoroughly trained to redress his wound, we once again bid our goodbyes to the amazing staff. They had seen us at our worst and had stuck with us, cheering us on and comforting us when needed. We will never forget the surgeon who so delicately repaired Benny's lungs. He is still often in our prayers and although we no longer have a need to see him, he stays in our hearts each day, in the living breathing boy called Benny.

FOURTEEN

Music, the Language of Benny's Soul

"HELLO! WE HEARD BENNY was having a bad day, so we rounded up the troops and our guitars to come play and sing for him," the welcome package arriving at our door in the form of Mervin Shrocks and their children equipped with their instruments was a happy sight.

The Shrock family had moved into our area when Benny was only a year old. We had asked them to sing at Benny's birthday party bash, and they moved to our community soon after that. They were some of our most dependable friends who were there at the drop of a hat to try to cheer Benny with their amazing talent of music and singing whenever word would reach their ears that he was sick.

These jamming sessions with the Shrocks showed us that music was a rich and beautiful way to connect with Benny. We found out that when we sang to him, he was calmer. He let us know what his favorite songs were by fussing if we sang one he didn't like. At church he often put his head against our throat to feel the vibrations from our vocal chords. If the congregation sang a song too soulful, he would cry so hard we had to take him out. He loved when we sang and danced with him to upbeat songs.

Ain't nobody named Benny got no time for slow songs, no sir, they must be high energy and exciting. He is my speed! I don't like many slow songs either.

When Benny was on the verge of a meltdown, we would sing into his ear and quickly dissolve the inconsolable stream of tears that had been about to occur.

I love my Benny, oh yes I do,
I love my Benny, Oh yes it's true,
When he's not with me, I'm blue,
Oh Benny I love you.

Sometimes we were too late and the episode was too far along to stop. We were being educated with a capital "E" on Benny language and Benny meltdowns.

"The waiting room is completely full, Hannah. Let's just park the wheelchair here inside the door and wait for a space to open up," I instructed as we walked into the GI doctor's office for a checkup.

Benny started crying the minute he realized his ride was over and that all eyes were on him. He knew very well that he was the object of curious stares, and he did not appreciate it the tiniest bit. Benjamin was completely over and done with this visit a few minutes after arriving.

Not a single song got him over it, probably because we sang so quietly in his ear that he couldn't even hear it. We had no desire to give out a free solo concert to the waiting room audience. I am confident in many things, but singing in front of people is not one of them. And so we took Benjamin back outside, dried his tears, assured him all was well, and sang "Jesus Signed My Pardon" loudly and clearly in the parking lot where no ears could be harmed by our scary voices. And then he was over it and we went back inside to the overstuffed room and waited our turn.

"Benny I made you a little guitar out of a Kleenex box and rubber bands! Let's see you play it. Here, take it, Benny Boy," voiced Laurie excitedly as she handed the lowly guitar to Benny.

His eyes sparkled and shone as he picked it up and promptly started strumming. What?

"Oh my goodness, Mom, look! He even knows how to hold it!" exclaimed Laurie, grinning from ear to ear. "You're so smart, Benjamin!"

That was ten years ago, and ever since that moment he is rarely seen without a toy guitar in his hands. They are toys; they break. We have probably gone through at least 15-20 mini guitars or ukuleles since then. We cannot live without them!

One melodic sound that bothers Benny, is listening to his family eat corn on the cob.

"Come and get it while it's hot!" I announced, carrying the platter of steaming, buttery, yellow corn to the table. "Doesn't this look so delicious?"

"Mmm, we can't even wait to sink our teeth into it!" exclaimed the girls in delightful anticipation, quickly smearing their golden ear of corn with butter and generous amounts of salt before putting it to their watering mouths and chomping down as politely as possible.

"Whoosh, whoosh, whoosh!" The trach-whooshed cries reverberated across the table as all heads swiveled in Benny's direction at his wail of fright. Then he stopped crying long enough to carefully look all around the table at everyone devouring that yummy corn and let out another trach-whooshing scream.

"Benny, what's wrong?" asked Maynard.

"I think he's scared to see and hear us eating corn!" I exclaimed in dismay.

"Well that's too bad, I'm eating corn on the cob anyway," declared Laurie.

"Me too!" stated Diana emphatically, "He just has to be scared this time around."

Hannah and Sammy were too busy to notice and went right on eating.

I must defend us here. We are generally polite and mannerly at meal time. Even when we eat corn on the cob, we don't hog out and sound like pigs feeding. Not even Maynard, who was raised with six sisters. They would never have allowed him to be so uncivilized.

"He's not having it," sighed Maynard. "I will take him in the living room and start his music DVD so he won't have to listen to us all eating our corn."

And so that is how we ate corn from then on out. To this day he gets upset when we eat corn! We either have to put him "away" to watch a music DVD, or have him sob throughout the whole meal.

We have bought and worn out music DVDs like no other family ever has, I'm sure. We first discovered his love for music DVDs one day when the girls were watching a preview of "Alvin and the Chipmunks" on the internet.

As the "Chipmunks" started singing, Benny's eyes lit up and latched on the screen, busting out in trach giggles that made him cough enough to require suctioning. I came running to see what had inspired this joy.

I excitedly called Maynard, to tell him the new thing Benny had discovered, "Benny busts out into giggles whenever Alvin and the Chipmunks sing!"

Laurie was always my technical girl. When she took naps or went to bed, my computer skills also went night-night. She was and still is often called upon to fix our "internet thing" issues. So it was Laurie who decided to see what else he liked to watch. It started a music marathon at the Troyers.

Benny likes predictability and routine. If these are absent he is a terrible mess. Because of this, he would latch on to one group of singers and them only. In his little mind they were the one and only vocals remotely acceptable to listen to. When we got so weary of one group that we knew we would lose our minds and pull out our abundance of long hair if we heard them even one more time, we had to slowly and with much clapping and childish antics get him to accept a different singer.

"Maynard, Benny has a heart echo next week. Will you be able to go with me?" I asked tentatively.

"Yes, I should be able to go along. Make sure you have "River of Jordan" downloaded on our phones. It's the only way he will endure the echo without screaming the entire time," advised Maynard.

"Sure enough. I wouldn't dare go without it," I agreed.

The next week as we pulled into the plush cardiology unit, we were thankful we had discovered that music helped Benny cope even at doctor visits. The echo went more smoothly than liquid gold honey running down our throats. We kept the little flip phone firmly tucked by his ear, so he could hear Jeff and Sheri Easter crooning "River of Jordan" the whole time.

"Benny, Boo Boo, you were such a good boy today!" exclaimed the cardiologist with a smile. "That music really helped. Don't come without it ever again!"

As they wrapped things up, the doctor turned to us with a triumphant glow. "Everything still looks great! No surgery for Benny Boy anytime soon. I will see you in six months just to check him out again. Bye, Benny. Where's Benny, Boo Boo? I'm going away now, Benny!" and I heard him sing as he walked out of sight, "Oh the River of Jordan...and the cool waters cleansed my soul!"

The nurses giggled with delight, snapped their fingers and danced little jigs as they joined in, "Oh the River of Jordan, what a beautiful song! I can't believe he likes music so much. That must be a lifesaver!"

We heartily agreed that it was. I just bet Jeff and Sheri Easter have no idea how much their singing helped these special needs parents. Or how they have blessed and touched the dearest soul I know, my Benny Boy. I only hope he can meet them some day, like he met Conrad Fisher.

Conrad Fisher personally took the time to meet Benny and to shake his hand after a local concert. He even got right down on Benny's level, slapping his own hat onto Benny's head, talking to him nonstop, even though Benny could not utter a word back. It's people like this that make the special needs world go around. Conrad's music is gospel/country and he is a high energy performer. When Benny watches music videos produced by Conrad, he is right up against the screen, making sure he sees everything, playing his ukulele like he is one of the band. When Conrad sings "Home from the Sea," Benny goes completely still, and it's like his heart and soul are traveling places we could never afford to take him.

Another favorite group of his is Celtic Thunder. When they start singing "A Place In The Choir", Benny yells for someone to come join him to dance and clap with him.

These downloaded songs went with us when Benny was six years old as we made the trip back to Rainbow Babies to remove his trach. His jaw had been ready for awhile, but it was the repeated lung infections that caused Benny to end up on the ventilator and caused the treatment to be postponed.

"Once he has stayed off the ventilator for two years we will remove the trach completely," Dr. Decker had said.

At the time it had seemed like this would never happen, but here we were. Yes, we were at this stage of Benny's life and we could hardly breathe, we were so excited to have it behind us.

We watched once again as Benny disappeared behind the cold steel doors of the operating room. We walked to the sitting room apprehensively to wait the moment he would return to us.

When the doctor came out to us after surgery to remove the trach, he had such a defeated look that we thought something terrible had happened.

"When Benny was starting to come out of sedation, he coughed before I was ready. I had just finished stitching, and was just tying it all up when he coughed. This opened the stitch back up, and blew the air from his cough up under his skin. Oh, he looks awful, Mrs. Troyer, I am so sorry. This only happens every once in a while. He will be fine, but his face looks like a blown up balloon. Oh, here he comes now."

My eyes popped, and I gasped in shocked horror at the size of Benny's head. He indeed looked like a blown up balloon, except a balloon is smooth. Benny's face was perfectly blown up in some places, and then he had normal pockets here and there that were not blown up. It reminded me of lumpy bread dough rising unevenly in a bowl.

Dr. Decker put his arms around us and walked back with us apologizing profusely the whole time.

"Dr. Decker, it will be okay, it wasn't your fault. We will sing to him and he will be comforted." We tried to make him feel better as Maynard quickly picked up Benny and started singing "Jesus Loves Benjamin, This I Know." When that didn't work, we whipped out the phone and played his downloaded songs and he settled right down.

"Yes, it will be okay and it will go away in about twenty-four hours, but I did not want this to happen to my Benny Boy."

lamented Dr. Decker regretfully. "We will get you a room in PICU and keep him for one extra day, just to make sure nothing else turns up."

After a two day stay, we were on our way home, eager to begin our brand new trach-less life. It was strange to not be suctioning all the time, and many times I found myself reaching for the catheter that was no longer there, when Benny faltered at not understanding what to do with the air that all went up through his nose and mouth now, instead of through his trach. He adapted quickly, though, and we enjoyed our new found freedom.

Whenever there were bands at the local fairs that we deemed acceptable, we took Benny to enjoy the Ferris wheel, the carousel and the music. He would scream and kick and laugh through the whole concert. At one such concert a lady had stare eyes. Those eyes locked down on Benjamin and would not stop staring as she sipped at her high calorie coke, adding even more plush to her already plump figure.

"Just ignore it, honey, it's fine. Benny is having so much fun. The good thing about an outdoor concert is that it's so loud, nobody can even hear him. Go, Benny!" encouraged Maynard with a grin.

After the concert the stare lady sauntered up to Benny. *Oh no, what is she going to say*, I wondered as a prickle of unease came over me.

"I just loved your dancing, little boy! It was perfect. God bless you, sweetheart." She smiled at us and gave Benny a hug before she walked away.

Benny's tiny converse shoes had not once left his wheelchair to dance across the floor but he had danced with the purest of joys right there in his chair all evening.

While I had been miffed and had judged the woman so quickly, she had understood Benny's heart. I was smitten with remorse so great that I could feel the weight of it the rest of the evening.

This little episode taught me so much. It taught me to quit assuming the worst, to stop looking for negativity, and to not think everyone that stares is being ignorant or rude. Plus, Benjamin is just downright cute. What's not to stare at and love?

Our local church has been phenomenal with Benny. They allow Benny to be Benny. Whether it's good or bad, we know it is okay at church, and we are safe with these people. It means everything to us.

Benny claps and giggles loudly during the service. Sometimes the outburst is at a very awkward moment. Other times it is perfect. He loves when babies cry, and will break into gleeful laughter. Benny greatly enjoys the moment of discomfort at the expense of frazzled mothers, quickly exiting with a screaming baby.

One Sunday morning, a few minutes into the worship service, Darien announced with a smile, "Okay, at this time I invite Benny to come up and help play his favorite songs."

Benny's ears perked up at his name and wonder of wonders, he was wheeled up front by his daddy and they headed straight for the most awesome instrument in the world.

As we slid into Benny's favorite songs, Darien held the guitar and fingered the chords while Benny went completely crazy. He strummed with his long delicate fingers as if it was the last thing he would ever do and he wanted to make sure it was impressive. The congregation began to clap and drove Benny even wilder while they laughed and sang along with him.

Whenever Maynard preached, Benny used to go up and sit next to the pulpit, because he would be naughty for me when Maynard wasn't sitting beside him in the audience. He always signed "water" to a certain brother because he knew he would get Maynard a cup while he preached, and Benny thought he needed one, too. Then he sat there and sipped his water and watched Maynard preach. This all went well and according to plan, until he got older and he discovered that he could make people laugh with his hilarious antics up front, especially when he singled out his favorite people and blinked furiously fast at them. This was a trick the girls had taught him.

One day after church, we heard of a live play in our local town. They were showing *Helen Keller*.

"I think this would be worthwhile to see," I told Maynard.

"You and the girls take a day off and go, and I will stay home with Benny," offered Maynard generously.

"Really? You're sure?" I quizzed.

"Yes, of course I'm sure. You go have fun and Benny and I will have even more fun taking a nice long Sunday afternoon siesta."

"Okay, we will!" I gushed.

I had no idea the life change I was about to experience. I watched Annie Sullivan as she calmly but assertively got the blind and deaf Helen to mind by telling her the same thing over and over. Annie did not accept anything less than what she was asking Helen to do. Helen was not allowed to reach into Annie's plate of food and eat from it. Over and over Annie sat Helen back down on her chair at her own plate, placing the spoon back in her hand urging her to eat that way. Annie did not get angry when food was thrown smack into her face. To see it acted out live brought such clarity and direction to my life that I could hardly wait to try it on Benjamin. I cried throughout most of the play. It was so real and spoke directly to my soul. What if I could make Benjamin mind in the little things? Hair pulling, phone grabbing, slamming any door he could find...there were so many annoying little things that I thought I just had to accept as my life.

So the next time during church, when Maynard went up to preach, I kept Benny by my side. Oh, he did not like it one little bit! He grabbed at my blouse, my sleeve, my hand; he grabbed anything he could think of to make me take him up to Maynard. I calmly and assertively placed his hand back on his chair each time. We went back and forth in this fashion more times than I could count. Suddenly, he stopped his tugging at me. He accepted this as the new normal and sat contentedly throughout the rest of the service. It was an absolute miracle!

One musical thing I cannot break him of is an act of pure fine-tuned art that he insists on at the most awkward moments he could possibly find. He is so talented that it's almost like he knows what he's doing. Some people call it cutting the cheese. Others say breaking wind, bottom burps, polluting the air, shooting a fairy, tooting, or passing gas.

Here is one example of his raw skill. One evening we had the whole church at our house for homemade ice cream and waffles. Oh, my, was it amazing! Of course we would pray for a blessing on the food before eating, asking God to kindly obliterate any calories and fats that might want to cling onto the waists of over the hill folks.

"Danny, would you pray a blessing on the food tonight?" asked Maynard.

"Sure," replied Danny, "Let's pray. Dear heavenly Father, thank you for this evening of fellowship and food... (Insert the sound of Benny letting one slip into the silence)...and um, thank you, Lord ... (insert the sound of Benny really letting it rip into the now alert silence)... yes, Lord, and thank you for this food... (Danny overheard the four sisters behind him snorting and trying to suppress giggles and couldn't help but erupt in giggles himself)...and that's an Amen!"

And just like that the whole houseful of people exploded into loud guffaws and yelps of laughter.

"Go, Benny! You're the bomb!" exclaimed Danny.

"Look at Marietta, she's bright red! Been out in the sun lately?" The bantering back and forth was all in good fun and love. We have an amazing brotherhood of fine people at our fellowship who have a generous sense of humor.

This is how Benny keeps the ice broken, making sure our local church group stays alive and kicking, and no one ever falls asleep during prayers. There is no pretense in Benny. Everything he does is exactly how he is and he offers no apologies.

Like I said, I have not even tried to break him of this one. I have had many setbacks along the way since then in breaking him of his other issues. It is a daily challenge and it takes consistency. I was not born with an everlasting supply of patience like my good, kind husband. My storehouses are often empty and I work insanely hard at stocking even a tiny supply of patience.

My idea of life before I had Benjamin was *wham, bam, thank you ma'am. Git er done or git out. Anything worth doing is worth doing right; but fast! Top speed old girl!*

Benny has taught me to slow down and listen to the music around me. He has taught me a new meaning to the cliché that our children keep us humble. Tooting into silent rooms will humble me every single time, but I can laugh about it now. He has taught me about acceptance and unconditional love. He has taught me by the way he responds to people, what is in their hearts, whether they be critical, kind or good.

He is my Benny, and his heart is bigger than anyone else I know.

FIFTEEN

The Unconditional Love of Benny

BY WRITING OUR STORY I feel vulnerable and exposed. I am well aware that I have put myself in danger of skeptics. I am reluctant to wave goodbye to the bliss of a private life, but if I can encourage only one other family who is walking the bewildering special needs trail for the first time, it will be alright.

Little Benny Boy changed our whole life. We had no idea the ride we were about to begin the day he was born. We had no idea how we would become things we never dreamed possible, such as a doctor, a nurse, an advocate, a therapist, specialist, superman, super woman and super siblings. We would learn that it is possible to walk hand in hand with joy and grief, to know all is not okay and yet be able to go on. Adding a sense of humor to the journey helps tremendously.

We didn't even know it that stormy day, but when we officially became special needs parents on July 8, 2003 we also became all the above. We were so innocent that sometimes I can't even remember what the days had been like before little Benny popped into our lives.

A new way of life filled with medical vocabulary became commonplace, and professional doctors in long white lab coats teach us foreign words with strange meanings. It is a life where we get asked a bazillion questions, and we have a gazillion more of our own.

Did God ever give us more than we could handle? The reality is yes, he did. But it is only so that he can show his grace to be sufficient. There were many moments I couldn't believe in his grace, but in time I got there. God is good and helps us take one little day at a time.

As people watch us prep Benny for the night, or set up his feeds, or sit in the hospital for weeks on end, they often tell us that they could never do what we do. I have news. I can't either. I get hot and faint all over sometimes when unexpected things happen like when his trach would come out or his feeding tube would be yanked out by some curious, innocent child, or the times he would need to be "bagged" (which still terrifies me to the core), and I "can't" do it, but somehow I do!

First of all, it's not true that others couldn't do what we do. I know anyone could. Maybe not everyone has a special child like Benny given as a gift; therefore, they can never know that they could have been able to do it.

Secondly, we don't have a choice. We often hear that God only gives special children to special people. Believe me when I say that we are not special or extraordinary for having Benjamin born to us. We are his mommy and daddy! How could we possibly not go above and beyond in our care for him? Special needs children are not reserved for only the chosen few. They appear everywhere whether we are Hollywood stars, major league players, famous singers, a millionaire, neighbors, relatives or friends. Each one would love their child to pieces and embrace this call on their life.

My take on it is this: I am the most blessed mom in town for having a child named Benny in my life. Benjamin is not a tragedy or a bother. Benny loves life and he laughs and dances in his chair with pure joy just like other children. His unique personality and character keeps me on my toes. He has likes, dislikes, opinions, and a sense of humor. He has an infectious laugh, and a temper, but most of all he is bestowed with a capacity to love that is unparalleled to any I have ever known.

When I found out I had a special needs child, I purposed in my heart these three things:

*Benny will smell good

*Benny will be clean

*Benny will wear nice clothes

This is the most important calling I have on this earth. God gave me this work, and I embrace it with my whole heart. I don't get much else done, but I am fulfilling this very special assignment! In return, I have a child that loves me unconditionally. No matter what, he is always happy to see us all. Benny's unconditional love beats everything I have ever known about being loved and loving others. I don't even know how I would survive my life without his beautiful loving soul.

When we have hard days, we gravitate to Benny, reach down and pick him up and his sweet love heals so many of our hurts, whatever they may be. Even today when he is 14 years old, and barely fits on our laps we still draw that special love from him. I have seen all my daughters do this, and I don't think they even realize that Benny just mended some pain inside their beautiful, unselfish, giving hearts. We are so utterly blessed with this incredible little person named Benny, and four daughters who love and care for him just like he was their own.

Because this road may be lonely, we must find those friends who take our hand and patiently travel with us without passing judgment. We need friends we are safe with. We may be a hard lot to understand, but we cannot do this alone. At the beginning we thought we could make everyone understand our life, but we soon knew this was not so. We were on a path so unique that we had to come to a place where we were okay with others never "getting it."

We as parents to special needs kids are called to live a life of forgiveness. People are well meaning and innocent even when they make remarks that sting. I was one of those very souls before I had Benny. I was on the outside looking in and didn't understand how to respond to such parents either. We must never let this hinder our journey.

Because our hearts as special needs parents are already broken, it is so easy to allow ourselves to become a wounded soul, and invite even more hurts to unnecessarily harm us. We must choose to let joy and laughter ride along with the brokenness.

For the longest time I walked around as a broken, crippled woman. I didn't allow myself the liberty of acknowledging that I was a different mother. I thought I had to keep up all appearances and participate in functions just like all "normal" moms do. I felt I should be able to cook a full course meal for 50 people and still take care of Benjamin. I felt I needed to have large events at my house like before, no matter that I could barely get it done. The gardens I put out were vast, green, gigantic, overwhelming monsters I thought I must do anyway. I canned and froze garden proceeds as if preparing for YK2 every single year.

The problem with all this was that because I thought I had to do everything like before, plus take care of Benjamin, others expected it of me, too. It wasn't anyone's fault but my own.

If there is anything I could go back and tell my young, thirty some squirt self it would be *stop. Stop it right now. You don't have to do all this. You have Benjamin to take care of and four daughters to home school. You have three full time jobs right there. Home school. Benjamin. Home maker.* And if I would not listen to myself, then I would take me and somehow knock some sense into me until I minded, and slowed down. I would make sure that I would understand how to say no. And because my husband and I both have issues with saying no, I would next tackle Maynard, and make sure he learns.

To my great and terrible shame, it took me a long time to finally allow myself to take a break and admit it as a right because of Benjamin. I look at it as a phase in the education from my master teacher named Benny. That was a long phase. What can I say? I'm a slow learner in life lessons.

Benny taught me to unlearn virtually everything that had made me, me. He rearranged my priorities, making me a secure and stronger person. In the last few years I have not canned one jar of garden produce. I have not even had a garden for two years. I buy fresh strawberries instead of raising my own. Oh, my! This non-gardening thing has been difficult for me to learn. I rarely bake my own bread now. I don't have a full meal on the table every single evening. I have eased off on my OCD tendencies to clean. When friends head off on cruises and tours, I might still get an "F" on this subject sometimes because it's so hard to let go of. But I am learning to be content at home when others go on vacation. The last thing I clung to and reluctantly released was perfect flower beds. The lessons I have learned from Benny have hurt more than just about anything else, but every single one has been worth it a thousand times over.

Benjamin's love of life is purer than the purest, snowflake God ever designed. He lives his life for the moment. He loves to laugh. He laughs at loud noises or when anything gets dropped accidentally. He thinks it is hilarious to hear coughing. He laughs like he is being tickled all over when he is sitting on my lap and I blow my nose. He lays his head against my cheek to get every vibe from so gross an act. His laughs are so contagious, so belly deep, so pure and true that he soon has everyone within earshot hooting along with him.

Benjamin's vocabulary consists of one entire word: Mom. I am highly honored. That being said, we have also taught him some sign language. He can let us know when he wants water, milk, a tube feed, a movie, his guitar, his mom, his dad, each individual sister, a puppy, a baby, turn the lights on, turn on the fan, I want to go night-night, (which is basically never), put me in my wheel chair and turn me loose, change my diaper, sing a song for me, *no, not that song*, please, thank you, and your welcome.

He worries about only one thing. Going to school. He does not like to leave the safety of his home and his fellow servants for an entire day. We sent him anyway for six long years. He had amazing teachers and an awesome staff at school, but it seemed he never connected. They tried so hard, and loved our Benny to pieces. When the seventh year rolled around, I pulled out all the stops and said *this is it. No more.* Our hearts could not bear another year listening to him weep every single morning as he peered over the edge of the bathtub with his puppy brown eyes and worriedly checked whether we laid out jeans or pajamas. If he saw blue jeans, he started crying right away, and cried until he was going up the lift of the big yellow school bus. The sting of betrayal on his broken facial expression crushed our heart every time as they took him away.

To be totally honest, when I look at what our dreams had been for our future, it had not included a child living with us when we were old and beautiful with gray hair and dentures, rocking on squeaky chairs on the front porch. But now I can't imagine life without Benny. He fills us with joy and makes our house ring with laughter. Benny will be with us for as long as he lives. I only pray we will be able to care for him always. No matter what, we will never stop fighting for him and believing in him, cheering him on in life.

Living with Benny, taking care of his medical needs, and loving Benny with my heart and soul has helped me stop and smell the flowers along the way. He has taught me to look at things through brand new eyes. He is our Bubby. He has the great and terrible ability to make or break our days. Benjamin leaves footprints in our hearts and we will never be the same. Thank God. We are blessed. We love our life. We love our family. We love our Benny.

"God never promised days without pain, neither laughter without sorrow, nor sun without rain, but he did promise; *strength* for the day, *comfort* for the tears and *light for the way.*"

-*Annie Johnson Flint*

SIXTEEN

Special Needs Siblings Speak Out

The sibling love between Benny and the girls goes beyond anything I ever expected. When they take pictures with Benny, there is an extra sparkle in their eyes because of the overwhelming joy of loving a brother named Benny.

Here are their stories.

DIANA

I remember feeling completely incredulous when Dad announced to us four girls that we had a baby brother. A baby boy? It seemed unreal. I had been expecting another sister because that's how it had always been before. He was such a cute baby and we all fought to hold him and love on him right from the start.

My memories of seeing him at the hospital the first time are actually pretty fuzzy. I do remember feeling a little bit freaked out at walking into his hospital room and seeing all the tubes and monitors blinking away. After a while the tubes, wires and monitors weren't scary anymore.

I was so relieved when he came home from the hospital. It felt like a weight fell off my shoulders to finally have Mom and Dad home again, and not to be traveling back and forth between home and the hospital all the time. It was by no means easy. Benny had to be watched all the time and had tubes and monitors everywhere. There were some humorous dashes to the bedroom when an alarm would go off, only to find a tube had detached and Benny was sleeping peacefully. We had so much fun holding him again. At the hospital we had to take turns and work around all the machines and just getting him out of his bed was a big fuss, so it didn't happen as much as we would have liked.

I honestly can't remember when the realization hit me that we were a special needs family. I'm sure it happened, but I've become so used to living as a special needs family that I don't really remember what it was like before we had Benny in our lives.

Having a special needs sibling has taught me so much. I don't know if I can even put it into words but I will try. For one thing, it has made our family really close because we all work together to care for him. It has helped us all to grow up and to take on responsibilities that lots of other kids our age have never had. Best of all, he taught us that people with handicaps and disabilities are people just like everyone else. Actually, I've learned that many times the people with handicaps often excel in areas that we so-called "normal" people are handicapped in. For example, Benny is so good at reading people's spirits. He can tell if someone is genuine. He is so good at loving the people in his life unconditionally. I can't tell you everything he's taught me, but he has been a great teacher in all the important things like loving people, seeing things from a different perspective and giving and expecting nothing in return.

To any special needs siblings out there, I just want to let you know that you are awesome, you've got this, and even though it's hard sometimes and it feels like none of your friends really get it, it's okay because the rewards and blessings you get in return totally outweigh all the icky stuff. You've been handed an incredible chance to learn what selfless service is really like, and most of all you've been given a sibling who will love you in a way that nobody else can. So, dive right into this, love on your sibling and stick up for him or her. Be their best friend. And one more thing; it's okay if you need a break now and then. Go get a coffee or take a quiet time if you need it. And hey, you could make it possible for your parents to do the same thing!

LAURIE

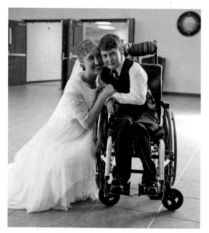

Some people might think that growing up with a special needs sibling would be a disappointment or a burden. I see it as an honor. My family and I were handpicked by God to be Benny's family and it doesn't get more special than that!

When he was born the excitement was high. We finally had a brother after 4 girls and we were absolutely thrilled! I remember holding him for the first time and being astounded at how tiny and adorable he was. I was smitten the moment I laid my eyes on him. We all were. We had no idea how drastically our lives would change the day he entered the world or how much of an impact he would have on our lives and on those around us.

The next few years were hard, but beautiful. In the midst of the pain of seeing Ben lying in hospital beds for weeks at a time with tubes and monitors everywhere, or of kissing him goodbye because the Doctors said he wouldn't make it through the night, or of having to grow up at 10 years old to help take care of my two younger siblings, or of missing Mom and Dad...in all that, I now see beauty in the broken mess that our lives were.

The beauty in the midst of all that and more was miracles! Miracles don't just happen to the people in stories you hear, they happen to the ordinary. They happen to the ones crying out in anguish and pleading to not have their little brother taken so soon. Having a prayer as great as those answered, is beauty. It made my faith so much stronger because I knew God was listening. He cared. He loved. Through all that it made me realize the importance of prayer.

I never wished that Ben would be a normal baby. To me, he was who he was supposed to be. He was who God made him and so he was perfect. I never understood why people would make fun or stare at him rudely. It made me angry. And there were times when tears were shed between us girls because we just couldn't understand how someone could say such horrible things about our precious little brother. He couldn't speak for himself or he couldn't tell people to stop staring at him. So, we became his protectors. We became his voice. It took some hard lessons for us to realize that most of the people staring were not doing it intentionally. The people mocking had no idea how special Ben is and how much they are missing out by not being with him and getting to know him.

Throughout the years Ben has taught me many things. One of these things is to be who God made you to be. We were made in God's image and if we all just accepted ourselves the way Ben does, we would all be so much happier. Ben is just who he is, like it or leave it. He can't walk, can't verbally speak, can't eat by himself, can't take care of himself at all, but he's happy.

To have Ben as my brother is one of the greatest blessings. I don't want to think who I'd be today if I wouldn't have him in my life. He's taught me compassion, grace, selflessness, joy, and much more!

I wish everyone had the opportunity to have a Benny in their lives.

The next time you see someone who is handicapped or special needs just go and talk to them. Even if you are scared out of your mind. Just do it.

HANNAH

When Benny was born I was a mere 5 years old. We were sent to Jon and Ellie's house so Mom could have her baby.

"Dad's here!" exclaimed Laurie.

Laurie dashed out to the van, leaping onto the running board even before it came to a halt.

"Is it a boy?" she asked excitedly.

"It's a boy!" answered Dad, jumping out and hugging us all as we surrounded him with questions.

We all piled inside the van quickly, and waited impatiently for Dad to stop talking to Jon. One of Jon's little girls stood at the van door jabbering away, caught up in the excitement of a three year old.

"Hannah, do you think your baby brother can already pick boogers?" She asked seriously and we all burst out laughing.

"No, he's a baby, he can't pick boogers yet," I answered, giggling.

"Dad! Hurry!" yelled Diana, sticking her head out the window.

When we were finally on the road, it only took about 3 minutes to get to our house. We all clambered out of the van, chattering like a bunch of monkeys as we ran for the bedroom. The house seemed dark without electricity, but no matter, we had a baby brother.

I waited with ants in my pants until it was finally my turn to hold Benjamin. Being the third in line, it was almost unbearable. I couldn't believe how tiny he was when he finally landed in my arms. I stroked his head of black hair as he stole a chunk of my heart right out from under me. I had a brother of my very own. I decided right then and there that I would always be there for him, and I would always look out for him. Little did I know just how much.

I don't recall anything of that awful doctor visit Mom wrote about. She says it's the grace of God, and she is glad I don't remember.

My memories of Benjamin being in the hospital the first time don't involve Benny much. I had more important things to accomplish. Namely, reaching the elevator button before anyone else, and landing the step stool beside Benny's bed before Samantha did. And, of course, I ate as many Popsicles as the nurses could possibly bring.

We always had to stop at the receptionist before entering PICU so she could take our temperature and look into our ears. One time she didn't let me in because I had a slight fever. I was very upset. *How dare she keep me from my baby brother*, I thought, all manner of retaliation sailing through my mind. Dad sat with me in the waiting room as I watched the doors close behind my lucky sisters.

When the good news came that Benny was coming home, we hung welcome home signs everywhere and waited for him to arrive. Finally the ambulance pulled into our driveway, and there he was. A tiny human form with a load of black hair on a full size stretcher, still hooked up to beeping monitors. He looked so stinking cute and I couldn't wait to get my hands on him to love him to bits.

Long into that first night I remembered the strange, new, sounds of the machines and monitors required to care for Benny. At first they seemed loud, but I soon got used to them and they lulled me to sleep each night.

I was trained to suction Benny once I was old enough. I felt like I had just won an Oscar the first time Mom let me suction all by myself. I was so proud that I could care for Benny in this way.

One day we all loaded up and headed for a wedding in beautiful Amish country. This is my first memory when I realized Benny was different from other children. When the wedding ceremony ended and we all gathered in the yard waiting to be seated at the reception, my heart was shattered into a million pieces, when suddenly we were surrounded by about ten little boys. They stared and punched each other then laughed mockingly at Benny. The hurt I experienced from this incident will live with me for the rest of my life.

I watched as my Mom, with much grace and kindness, engaged those little boys in conversation like nothing was amiss, when I knew her own heart was breaking. I could never in a million years have been so nice. I wanted to tell them to go away and never come back. Benny was my brother. From the first moment I saw him, I had pledged to always be there for him. Would it be awful of me to say my ten year old self wanted to punch them? In the name of Benny? That won't make it okay, I know, so today when someone stands in front of him like that, I just tell them to go away. As calmly as I can, and without growling and snarling, trying to live up to the example my mom left me on that memorable day of my young life.

As a little girl, it never occurred to me that we couldn't do the things most families did. I was right in there with the rest of the family, caring for Benny. But now that I've grown into a young woman, I understand that we did have a different life from other girls. It is hard at times. We don't have the freedom to sleep in, or go here and there at the drop of a hat. Often we are needed at home to help with Benny. But the special love of Benny makes it all worth every sacrifice we make.

I will protect Benny with all that is within me as long as I live. I love Benny with my whole heart. Benny loves me with his whole heart. He is my brother. My special Benny Boy.

SAMANTHA

When Benny was born, I was only three. So, as you can imagine, my memory is limited! But one thing I can still clearly remember is walking into the dark room and scrambling excitedly onto the bed to see my amazing, little, tiny, baby brother. The next moments were tender and sweet. All of us gathered around our precious Benny, singing *I'm a Little Miracle*.

I can't exactly summon the memory of seeing Benjamin in the hospital for the first time, but I do remember the hospital visits. After racing down the halls with my older sister, Hannah, to see who would reach the elevator first, the triumphant winner would have the honor of pressing the glorious buttons! Don't even get me started with the water fountains. Once we finally got to our floor, there was another race! It was a race for the step-stool that would lift us up to our baby brother. As we peered over the mattress at his tiny form with wires and tubes all around him, the machines beeped in the background. There he lay, with the blackest mop of hair. What a goldmine we would hit if we were allowed to hold him!

The day that Benny finally came home, we buzzed around the house with excitement. He was coming home! I still remember seeing that huge ambulance coming down our drive way. They brought him in on a gigantic stretcher. At first I didn't believe he was actually on it! All I could see was bundles of white, but where was my brother? Just as they passed I saw a wisp of black hair, stark in comparison to the white of the sheets and blankets.

175

I remember thinking how tiny he looked in that huge bed!

Being as young as I was, I realized that my family was different. But it was my normal. Of course I see the curiosity in people's eyes whenever we go out in public. But this is our life. I can't really remember life without my brother. It wasn't until I was in my teens that I realized that special needs siblings live different lives. Getting glimpses into my friends' lives was shocking. The way our lives differed was amazing. We had so much responsibility, caring for our little gift. Hard as it may be at times, I would never trade it for anything in the world.

One thing Benny has shown me, through thick and thin, is to always be you. No matter where we are, who we are with, Benjamin is Benjamin. He never changes for anyone. He wears his heart out on his sleeve. When he laughs, you hear it. When he's sad, you hear it! And that is one thing that I think we can all take a lesson from.

Benny has another special gift. Let's call it a soul thermometer. He can sense how you're feeling. If you're sad or mad he knows! He'll react instantly. If you're sad, he'll comfort you in his own little way. And if you're mad, well, let's just say he reacts to that as well!

There are a lot of things Benny has taught this family. We are ordinary people, called to live an extraordinary life, because of the gift God has given us. Yes, our lives may be different. But we all come together because of Benjamin, our own little angel. Our lives are circled around him, and even though it can be a challenge at times, we would never trade it for anything.

REFERENCES

Rice Hopkins, Mary. "Little Miracle." *Good Buddies*. 1991. CD.